My Journey through Hell

Karen Slater

Fortis
Publishing Services

First Edition 2020

ISBN-13: 978-1-9163212-6-7

Fortis Publishing
Kemp House
160 City Road
London
EC1V 2NX

This book is a true story. Names have been not been changed and all events have been portrayed as accurately as my human memory was able to recall.

About the Author

Karen Slater was born in Benwell, a rough, deprived area of Newcastle upon Tyne, to a mother who was battling her own rejection and shame and a father who was embroiled in alcohol abuse.

From the very beginning, as a child, she realized her environment was hostile and dangerous.

She became the scapegoat of her family's dysfunction; confused about why there was so much hatred in her tiny world and constantly told how useless she was, a label she carried through into her adult life. A victim of child abuse and domestic violence, she fought her own demons and sought solace in drugs, alcohol, and self-harm.

At age forty-nine, after a serious suicide attempt, she decided to write her book. This is her story.

To my children, I love you more than you will ever know.

Acknowledgements

Thank you to my family and friends who love me no matter how neurotic I can be. To the NHS for always patching me back together again and to the psychologist at Newcastle's RVI for refusing to give up on me. To my aunty and her family for supporting me through my darkest days and to the world of recovery people who always welcome me back and encourage my growth.

And to Ken Scott, my book coach who believed in me too and convinced me I wasn't as useless as perhaps I thought. If you think you have a book in you, reach out to Scotty!

www.kenscottbooks.com

1

Newcastle Brown Ale for the Hardy Working Class

Mam and Dad were two bitter and angry people, I realized this at a very young age. Our household wasn't a conventional place to grow up; it was the classic example of dysfunctionality. I knew exactly why Mam was an angry young woman because she never tired of telling us. 'I should have never married your dad,' she'd scream, 'he wasn't the one for me.'

She came out with this in front of Dad too. Mostly during their fights, which were almost a constant in our lives. 'I should never have fucking married you,' she'd bellow at him across the room as she flung an ashtray or a cup at him.

But mostly it was in her melancholy moments, sitting with the three of us, me and my young brother and sister, that Mam told us the reality about our father and why she had married him.

She married Dad to teach her ex a lesson. She had been engaged to a man she loved dearly, but he had cheated on her and fell in love with the other woman. Just like that, our mam's world came crashing down; her romance and dreams were over.

She told us the breakup left her very sad and hurt. But more than sad and hurt, she was resentful.

She was a barmaid and worked in The British Legion pub in Newcastle. Dad was a regular there. One night after a few drinks too many he told the man next to him that he was going to marry 'that one,' and pointed over to Mam.

The man laughed but Dad shouted out over the counter, 'Here Blondie, I'm going to marry you one day.'

Blondie? How much had he'd had to drink, she thought? She had short black hair and not a blond hair anywhere to be seen.

It wasn't a romantic courtship, the revenge was sweeter and so they married soon after, on the day England won the World Cup in 1966.

It was all a little farcical as their wedding ceremony was at the exact same time that England kicked off the second half against Germany. They had to keep stopping the ceremony and keep calling in their guests to come inside because they kept sneaking out to watch the match on one of the TVs in a shop window on Gosforth High street.

They moved into my father's parents' house, a two up two down in Clara Street, Benwell and I was born on 28th Dec 1967, weighing 6lb 3oz, with a head of golden-brown hair.

Apparently, I never stopped crying and Mam didn't know what to do with me. I secretly believe I cried because she didn't know what to do with me full stop. Mam and Nana didn't get on very well, Nana thought being a barmaid wasn't an appropriate job for her son's wife and Mam liked to flirt a lot with the regulars. As tensions mounted, we upped and left to a flat of our own in Etal Lane in a suburb of Newcastle upon Tyne.

It was a two-bedroom maisonette and we lived on the middle

floor. Three years later my sister came along. Mam thought she looked like a doll and she would tell anyone who listened, 'Doesn't she look like a little dolly?'

She was petite with jet-black hair and dark brown eyes.

Doll or not, we still got chased out to play as soon as we could walk and we were not welcomed back until teatime.

Our parents drank every evening and if we were good, on a Friday, they'd insist we had a taste too. We were allowed half a glass of Dad's brown ale and I must admit I thought it was great. It wasn't a nice taste, but I did like how it warmed my belly.

My sister was still in her nappies when she experienced her first taste of brown ale and promptly spat it right across the room much to the amusement of Mam and Dad. After a few more tries she eventually got used to it and learned to keep it down.

Mam and Dad fought regularly, almost perpetually, one fight inevitably led to an argument and then another fight. It was an exceptionally strained marriage from the very start. Getting married to teach an ex a lesson is never really a good foundation for a family or a happy ever after.

The more it deteriorated into violence the worse it became for us kids. By now our little brother was born and that completed the family.

We were now a family of five, two violent and angry adults and three children under the age of six. It was volatile to say the least, aggressiveness fuelled with bitterness and copious amounts of Newcastle Brown Ale and vodka.

There was no love in our house, no kisses or cuddles or even kindness. It was just ridicule, violence and screaming.

Mam was angry all the time. She was angry with us and angry with Dad and flew into a rage sometimes for no apparent reason and woe betide any neighbours who found themselves on her wrong side.

The neighbour above us was a nice enough woman but for some reason one day she stuck up her two fingers at Mam as she left for work. Mam was furious and chased after her but when she had turned the corner at the top of the street, the neighbour had disappeared.

Mam wouldn't let it lie. She stewed and raged the whole day, waiting by the front door until she heard the woman come home. We all stood around wondering what was going to happen. Mam made no attempt to usher us into the kitchen out of sight to protect us from the inevitable violent scene. We stood behind her as she flung the door open and confronted our neighbour. The woman was in the middle of the stairwell and Mam grabbed her by her trench mac and launched into a completely unprovoked attack as the poor woman protested her innocence. I stood there terrified, begging Mam to stop but she wouldn't listen. She literally beat the shit out of her in our passage. As the woman begged for mercy and fell to the floor the attack continued until Mam was so exhausted, she couldn't hit her anymore. Mam fell to her knees beside the whimpering woman.

The woman was groaning and crying, there was blood all over the place and she had been beaten so badly I hardly recognised her. Her eyes were closed, already a mix of purple and black with two fat lips and a nose which was clearly out of shape. Mam pushed us inside and closed the door.

'That'll teach her to tell me to fuck off,' she said.

Not long after the police came to talk to Mam. Strange how we were allowed to witness the fight yet ushered away now the police were there. I don't know what happened exactly, but we were told we couldn't live there any longer and soon after we were moved to a house in New Vale Road, Fenham.

It was a three-bedroom house with our own garden. It looked like a lovely place to live. I wondered with a change of house, perhaps our parents would change too.

Me and my sister joined a jazz band, and for a while at least, there was little violence. We walked to school on our own, it was a long way and I carried a key around my neck to let us in on our return.

We loved school; we loved anything that took us out of harm's way. The jazz band training was the highlight of my week, Dad used to drop us off at Fawdon and we practiced for one or two hours every week. I looked forward to it so much; a few hours of normality where all the people smiled and laughed, and nobody wanted to fight.

Sundays were also nice; we got to wear our Sunday best clothes and dry our hair by the fire and eat sandwiches and chocolate teacakes with Nana Mary, who was the kindest soul on God's planet. Mam wouldn't beat us when Nana Mary was visiting.

I hated my pet dog, a powerfully built German Shepherd that some people called an Alsatian. I could never work that one out. It was fully grown, and it bared its teeth, which reminded me of a row of sharp daggers. And its growl...menacing and threatening.

It wasn't always like that. When Dad first brought it to the house it had soft eyes. It played with me and never growled, chased after tennis balls and pinched food from my fingers. I loved it. Not now.

Our family dog was now Dad's guard dog and it had me cornered in the sitting room by the door. It was a game my dad liked to play to prove he was a strong leader of our house. The reality was that we all knew who the boss was and that was our mam. She was undoubtedly the domineering force behind the power struggles and cruelty.

But Dad had found a new way to salvage a little of his pride, or so he thought. To me, even at such a young age he was nothing more than a vicious bully.

'Stand in the corner,' he'd order, 'and don't fucking move.'

It was Saturday evening and I was tired. He made me stand in the corner in my nylon nightie, the one that stuck to my skin with something called static.

He was reading The Evening Chronicle and he would speak to the dog. 'Watch your prey, watch the little cunt, Sheba, watch her.'

I was always a cunt. That was Dad's favourite word for me. In fact, it was Dad's favourite word for everyone.

Sheba did what she was told, she would growl and snarl and looked angry and stand on guard ready to attack me as soon as Dad said the word. He'd goad her; her hackles would stand up making her look even bigger than she was.

Dad would read the back page of the paper, all the while he would slip a few words to the dog. 'Wait Sheba, not yet, wait for my command.'

I knew what was coming and I was terrified. This game always ended the same way.

After a few minutes he would look up over the top of his paper and grin, 'Walk slowly to the other door Karen.'

The game had begun.

Like the dog I always followed Dad's orders. It was more than my life was worth not to and I knew that the attack that was about to come from the dog was the lesser of two evils. I would take tiny baby steps as slowly as I could in my bare feet, hardly daring to move any other part of my body or even breathe. It seemed to take forever to get to the other side of the room knowing that if I moved suddenly, the dog would be on top of me. Sheba was still sitting, alert, staring and growling, waiting for Dad's command. She was slavering at the mouth and I knew she was ready...poised. It wouldn't be long before Dad would say the words.

The tension was high, the room silent.

Dad was in his element; I could see that on his face, and he adored the control of having the huge beast of a dog obey him. And me too, I had to obey him. I was just another pawn in his warped game.

I'm almost there at the other side of the room. I wonder if this once I can make it to the door, open it and escape.

As I reach for the door handle, he shouts.

'Get her!'

The dog runs towards me and as she is just a few feet from me she leaps through the air and knocks me against the wall.

'No Sheba, no, leave me, leave me!'

'Get the cunt,' my dad repeats.

My body has been forced into the corner of the wall and I turn away to protect my face. The dog is biting the backs of my legs and my arms and is jumping up and down, growling and snarling, while Dad laughs and encourages her.

'Call her off Dad, call her off!'

'Stop whinging, you moaning cunt, she's only playing.'

It hurts, it hurts a lot, but Dad says she's only playing and if she really wanted to do some damage she would.

Playing or not, it still fucking hurts, the dog has drawn blood on my calf. It's a puncture wound, it's not deep but there's a lot of blood. I'm crying hysterically and begging Dad for mercy and I feel let down by Sheba because I was her friend and used to play ball with her a lot.

Sheba is hanging off my arm now, she won't let go, not until Dad says so and there is more blood running onto my nightie.

I don't know how long the game will be played. It depends what sort of mood Dad is in or how drunk he is.

Eventually he calls Sheba off and she goes over to where he is sitting, looking pleased with herself. I slide down the wall onto the floor. I'm shaking with fear, crying and sobbing and there are bruises everywhere and blood all over my nightie.

Dad is stroking Sheba. 'Clever girl,' he says, and I swear the dog is smiling at him, proud that she has done as she was told.

I'm tired and I don't want to play this game. I just want to go to bed where I'm safe and can use my imagination to take me to a better, safer environment. Dad laughs out loud. It's the only time he ever laughs these days and I'm pleased in a strange sort of way that I'm making him happy. It's better than making him angry and I know he won't set Sheba on me again. At least not tonight.

But I don't like this game. I'm glad it seems to be finished. Dad seems content...at peace. I'm rubbing at my wounds, but Dad tells me to 'Stop moaning,' and that 'She's only nipped you.'

The dog attacks were regular. Dad would even play his warped game in front of my Mam. I remember the first time it happened in front of Mam. She was reading a magazine on the sofa.

'Sheba,' Dad said.

It was his tone of voice. The only time he spoke like that to the dog was during his game.

'Watch her, watch the cunt.'

The dog started to growl and paced towards me.

'Mam,' I begged.

It was as if she didn't even know I was there.

'Walk slowly to the door,' Dad said.

'Mam, please.'

I was crying. Mam looked over the top of the magazine, looked at me and then the dog. And she went back to her magazine without saying a word.

The dog had me on the floor that time. I'd slipped and it was biting at my back and my bum while I screamed out loud.

Eventually Dad called Sheba off. I wiped the blood from my arms and the tears from my eyes and looked across the room. Dad was laughing demonically, and Mam's head was still buried in her magazine. Mam never rescued me. Besides, it meant Dad would leave Mam alone.

This was my young life for more years than I can care to remember.

I had a sadistic drunken father who had an angry German Shepherd and I had a cruel heartless mother who was worse than my Dad and the dog put together. She didn't know the meaning of the word 'nurture'. Only blame and shame and punishment.

I make my way to the bedroom, throw my blood-stained nightie to the floor and crawl into bed. I just want to pull the covers over my head, stay safe and warm and dream of being rescued. One day soon I will be a grown up then I won't feel so helpless.

I feel trapped, I'm scared of everyday life, frightened of what will happen next, constantly walking on eggshells. I'm existing, I'm not living.

Evenings are even worse than the mornings. My parents drink every evening, it's volatile. It is threatening and there's nowhere to run. I long for when they order me to bed. Bed and reading are my only escapes. I love reading, I escape in the fantasy of being rescued by a prince. One day I might even write a book myself.

I pray every single day and I can't understand where my God has gone. I have been a good girl and my teachers tell me so. I am good in my lessons and kind to my classmates. They say that God is good, that He will hear my prayers and that God loves his little children, 'Come on unto me and do not hinder them because the Kingdom of God belongs to little children,' Jesus said.

I sing the praises to God in assembly and I remember the words and even sing to Him quietly in bed. Have I not sung to Him enough, have I not prayed enough? Why does He not save me from this evil?

I still pray hard even though I'm angry at God. I pray because I'm terrified that He will make it even worse if I don't.

I don't think God can hear me; He's not listening. Perhaps He doesn't like this house, perhaps He doesn't like Newcastle?

2

Shamed and Humiliated

Dad was a bully, he'd walk around all tough out in the street and tell tall tales about people, but if ever there was trouble at the door, he would make Mam go and sort it out.

And sort it out she would. There was always trouble at our door. Many a scrap Mam had with people at the front door. Women mostly but sometimes men and sometimes both of them at the same time.

Dad never got involved in the fights at the front door or in the street. He felt more at home tormenting and beating up his children. Mam was tough, she had the measure of Dad, he feared her and because of this Dad would turn on me or my brother and sister. Mam would just sit or stand and look on saying nothing. You'd think our mother would come to our rescue, be all caring and kind, like the other nice mams in the street but she never did. She was the sinister one; she thrived on the drama and relished the cruelty. I saw it in her eyes many times.

She played the victim and yet she was the perpetrator, the attention seeker, the instigator, and she would often egg Dad on.

In the street she came over nice and friendly. She would force an insincere smile at people then squint her evil eyes. They looked even more evil in the cat's eyes glasses she wore. They narrowed her glare, made her look like a murderer out of a movie.

In the early days Mam and Dad would fight like boxers. The fights were fairly even at first. They'd shout and punch and kick and scratch but after a few minutes they'd both sort of call a joint truce. The fights would gradually get longer and longer, and it was more often Dad that would back down as Mam started to hit him with something or throw cups and ornaments across the room. Then the silence would follow, and they wouldn't talk to each other for days. They wouldn't talk to us either.

When Dad lost a fight to our mother us kids would know to get the hell out of his sight. Whenever he lost a fight you could guarantee he'd take it out on us.

Many times, he would snarl like the dog in our faces and punch us in the head for no other reason than Mam had just crowned him with a tea plate. He would constantly threaten to burst our lips and his favourite word would resurface.

'And you Karen, just a useless fucking thick cunt.'

They were both equally as savage in their beatings, but I would say Mam just edged it in the continued cruelty stakes. I often wanted the punches to miss my head and hit my eyes so at least I'd have something to show for it. I knew how sensitive the eyes were, how easily they turned black and blue and sometimes closed so that you couldn't see. Then hopefully someone would ask questions and I wouldn't need to keep any secrets anymore. I'd heard about kids who had been taken away from their parents. I prayed to God that someone would say something, and we'd get a new mam and dad, at least for a while.

No one ever asked. Not even the teachers when I turned up at school all scratched and dishevelled, sad and defeated.

It was an awful life of perpetual aggression. Day in and day out, I never quite knew what mood our parents would be in. I had to quickly learn how to scan our house and look for danger, read my parents' body language and listen to their tones to decide whether to be visible or not.

I don't know when I became the scapegoat or why, a projection of my mother's failings and entrapment to warrant marrying my dad. She never tired of letting me know that I was not wanted. The more I would try to win her love the more she would reject and punish me in exceptionally cruel ways.

Mam's favourite game was shame and humiliation. She enjoyed beating me in front of an audience, her friends, my friends, neighbours or the community, for little or no reason.

An incident that hurt more than most was at the local shops in front of the school kids. I was eleven when I was on the school bus coming home with my sister. There had been an incident at a bus stop and the bus had stopped for ten minutes. The school kids on the bus were complaining and shouting at the bus driver, 'Get going!'

The bus driver chucked a couple of lads off and we were on our way again. As the bus pulled up to our bus stop, I noticed Mam waiting on the pavement, which was unusual. I gave her a wave and a smile. She didn't wave back. She had her angry face on.

As I stepped from the bus, she launched herself at me. She grabbed me by the hair. 'You little bitch,' she squealed, 'I'll fucking kill you.'

She punched me repeatedly and threw me to the ground. What had I done? I couldn't understand it because I had been good at school, every one of the teachers had told me so.

It didn't stop. She kicked me on the ground and pulled me up by the hair. She hit me another few times and when I fell to the ground, she started to kick me again. I was aware of people trying to stop her and shouts from the other kids and eventually I just curled up in a ball pulling my hair tight around my head so she couldn't get a handful and pull me back to my feet.

She walked away and members of the public came to comfort me and my sister, who by this time was crying harder than I was because she had witnessed everything.

I had never felt much physical pain in the moment, only the pain of the humiliation of it all. All I felt was shame and embarrassment and that's what I never got used too.

Mam's switch for anger was like a thunderbolt of electricity and once it was switched on it couldn't be switched off until the voltage burned out or she was exhausted.

She just kept on beating me that day, she never let up, punching and kicking and pulling my hair until there was nothing left in her.

When I got home, I found out why she'd attacked me. She was late for work, so she had come looking for us. Mam had blamed me even though she had stood and watched the bus pull up to the bus stop, a bus that had been about ten minutes late because of an incident I had no power over.

There was always an audience and I'd sometimes hear some of them telling her to take it easy. Some would try and pull her off but most of them just stood and watched the entertainment. The shame. Oh God, the shame of people watching, and they all knew that I was a bad person because if I hadn't been so bad Mam wouldn't have battered me like that. The people at that bus stop hadn't known that Mam was hurting me because the bus was late. No, they were imagining far more sinister reasons why a parent was knocking seven bells out of their child.

The physical pain only registered afterwards. When the fear and adrenaline settled down the pain surfaced and became a reality.

It was the same after the dog attacks, after I went to bed and assessed the damage. The wounds throbbing constantly until eventually fatigue took over and I fell asleep.

Adrenaline is a wonderful thing, decreasing the body's ability to feel pain in the moment. It's as if I'm suspended watching the incident from above. However, the pounding sounds in my head were very real and so was the confusion, trying to figure out what the fuck was happening. The real pain and the real injury were the lack of love. Immeasurable.

Afterwards I would reflect, I would try to piece together the reasoning behind the beating of a child but there was no good reason. Both my mam and dad punched and kicked me like they would punch and kick an adult. It wasn't just a few slaps to the backside. I could never understand that. We were kids, not adults, and they battered all of us, but mostly I took the brunt. My sister was eight years old when she was prescribed beta-blockers for her nerves. My brother was five, he wasn't beaten so much at this age, but he witnessed everything. I sometimes think that was worse; my siblings were constantly afraid, always looking over their shoulders. I would take the beating, knowing that if I was getting battered then at least my brother and sister were okay.

But we were all victims, victims of bitterness and a distorted reality fuelled by alcohol. It was never going to be a great combination to raise a happy family.

I hated the smell of stale beer and smoke on them both. Lord knows how many times I had that foul breath down my throat, telling me how fucking useless I was.

No matter how hard I tried, nothing ever seemed right, or good enough for them.

At a young age Mam sat me down and taught me the basics of cooking, how to iron and how to clean and operate the hoover. Mam was apparently taking an interest in me, doing the things normal daughters and mam's do together. I enjoyed the cooking though I could never quite get the ironing right and cleaning was just plain boring. After a week or so I began to notice that Mam was getting less and less involved in the domestic side of running the house. More and more jobs were being put onto me and I was cooking Monday till Friday. Dad said it was expected of me, after all him and Mam worked.

They began to go out more too. Drinking in the house was no longer the done thing. I was more than capable of babysitting my brother and sister they said, so while they took themselves out early evening, I tidied the kitchen, washed up all the tea dishes and then got my brother and sister ready for bed.

Yet nothing was ever good enough. They always found fault.

Dad said the dinner was shite, the ironing was shite, everything was shite and we were all useless thick cunts.

He was right; looking back, our childhood was undoubtedly shite. Our parents were shite, our environment was shite and our life was shite.

I'd known this since the age of four, after an incident that would shape my view of myself and my world. I was playing outside with my friend when her mother noticed I was limping. I had been in a little pain for a few days but hadn't realised I was limping. The last person I would complain to about something was Mam.

This caring woman picked me up and said, 'Why are you limping pet?

'I dunno,' I said.

'Is your foot sore?'

'I suppose so.'

She carried me into her house and put me on the stairs to look at my foot.

She lifted it up to examine it. 'Oh dear.'

'What is it?'

She pressed into the sole in the middle of my foot and I nearly hit the roof.

'That's the spot,' she smiled, 'I'm sure there's some glass in there.'

'Glass?' I questioned.

'Yes, have you trod on any glass lately?'

Broken class was a constant in our house; broken glass from ornaments that Mam regularly threw at Dad, broken china from the cups and plates she hurled across the room. I was forever standing on broken bits and pieces with bare feet.

'Let's get you home to your mam, she can look at it and then we can get you to hospital if need be.'

I didn't want to go. I knew this would make Mam cross and I didn't want to be any trouble. My friend's mother was adamant Mam needed to see it. She clearly had never met my mam. She knocked on our door and I was nervous. Mam seemed polite and thanked the woman for her concerns and closed the door. Then the charm disappeared.

'For fuck's sake,' she shouted. 'As if I haven't enough to worry about!' She pinned me down to the kitchen floor, holding my little foot up to her eyes. 'I can't see anything,' she said, twisting my foot and leg where legs are not supposed to be twisted.

And then she pressed in exactly the same spot that the lady had pressed and I hit the roof for the second time that day.

'Oh, maybe there is something after all.'

'The lady said I might have to go to hospital to get it out,' I said.

She ignored me. Off she went to the kitchen drawers and pulled out a pair of tiny nail scissors, the type that are like miniature scalpels. I was still sitting on the kitchen floor as she lifted my leg. She looked at the sole of my foot again, pressed to make sure she had the right spot and dug the sharp point of the scissors into my flesh.

I had never experienced pain like it and screamed out as the shock at what had just happened hit me. It just infuriated her even more.

'Hold still,' she barked. 'For fuck's sake, hold still.'

The pain was incredible. She dug the scissors in again searching around for a shard of glass. She pushed harder and deeper creating a crater of raw flesh. The blood started to pool and run down my foot, dripping onto the floor which made it a hundred times harder for her to see. Her face was angry and contorted, as she pressed even further, I screamed and cried and pleaded.

'Please Mammy don't, you're hurting me.'

'Quit complaining,' she barked. 'I have to get it out, it's in there somewhere.'

She kept on digging and twisting the blade, pulling tight on my leg to get a better grip. The torture went on and at one point I thought I was going to pass out.

'I can see it,' she said, 'keep still.'

She dug the blades even further into my flesh as I screamed.

Eventually she found the piece of glass and pulled it out of my foot and held it up to the light, grinning. She seemed quite proud of her anaesthetic-free operation. She held the culprit between the scissor blades like a trophy. My foot was pulsating in pain, raw and wounded like my heart, the reality of my existence. The lack of even basic compassion was forever captured in that very moment.

As I stared into her eyes, I saw nothing more than a cruel woman. My mam. I was in shock; my foot throbbed in pain and I was still crying and incredibly hurt and distressed. She told me to 'shut the fuck up and go and play.'

She pushed me away.

'There's a plaster in the bathroom cabinet. Go put one on. It'll be fine in the morning.'

I couldn't speak between the tears, blood still dripping onto the floor.

'And clean that fucking mess up.'

I couldn't comprehend what had just happened. It was not a concerned or loving parent removing glass from her child's foot to ease the discomfort. No. She'd removed the glass because of the inconvenience of it all and she took the quickest possible option so that she could get on with what she had been doing. A trip to the hospital was never considered because the hospital was miles away and she would have to wait in a queue and there would be stitches and return visits and prescriptions and God knows what else.

I was only a child, desperate to be loved and yet I just knew from that moment on that it was always going to be like this. That was the day the penny dropped. I realised that my mother simply didn't care. I vowed to myself that I would stop trying to win her love. All I had ever done was to love my mam and try to prove what a good little girl I was in the hope she'd like me. She didn't even need to love me, liking me would have been enough.

I didn't know what mams were meant to be like, but I knew that this wasn't right. I wished the lady over the road who soothed me had been my mam. She was kind and caring. Or even my two Nanas, I had two Nanas who showed love and kindness. Why couldn't they be my mam?

There had never been any nurturing, care or gentleness. That day she blew out the light to my soul and I swore to myself that I wasn't going to bother with her ever again. Not ever.
The family dynamic was formed, I was the eldest and had become the scapegoat for my parent's projection of their own misery, their own reflection of hate and condemnation. It was never going to get any better. My sister was made the trophy and paid heavily for that title and my little brother became the invisible child. That was our blueprint.

We were all vying for some safety, some love, some comfort. Even our parents were, but they didn't know it. They were too busy scoring points and blaming anyone and everyone to notice that the house was a disaster, a fucking war zone with three casualties who were unable to escape.

3

Christmas, Season of Joy

The fighting continued and the drinking progressed to near-alcoholic proportions. Mam and Dad were sometimes permanently pissed and when they were pissed the fights would begin. To be honest, even when they weren't pissed, they were hung over and irritable, so either way there was always a tense atmosphere. There was constantly trouble looming on the horizon, another war simmering and bubbling just below the surface.

Sometimes Mam would say she'd had enough and that we were leaving Dad. We would up and leave Dad for days. We would be ushered out the front door with no prior warning to land on Nana Mary's (mam's mam,) doorstep, no time to get our teddies or belongings. Mam had already packed some basics and they were at the front door, with our coats, Mam hissing to Dad that she wasn't coming back, guess we weren't either. A lot of screaming in this family but no explanation...ever.

Although my dad could be very cruel, violent and horrible, it still cut me to pieces as we walked out of the door, suitcases in hand. Dad would be crying at the bottom of the stairs, pleading with Mam not to leave him. I knew how he felt, for as long as I could remember I had been shipped off to Dublin every school term holiday. I was a child, alone and feeling abandoned as I was dropped off at the airport and handed over to a chaperone that I had never met before. Lost and scared, my name pinned to my chest, wondering if I would ever return home to Newcastle. The relief of seeing a familiar face, my aunt's, at the gate after we landed. We were parted for weeks at a time. Defective, discarded, deserted.

Yes, I knew how my father felt as we were marched down the path.

I felt like a failure as a child, I felt I must be bad, born bad, a bad daughter. Even God and baby Jesus had deserted me because I couldn't get anything right. The more I tried to be good, the more erratic life became. I was moulded from uncertainty and fear. I knew that I had no control over my parents' fights. I didn't start them, and I certainly couldn't get them to stop, no matter how hard I begged them. The drunkenness either, I didn't start their drinking and I sure as hell couldn't get them to stop. A regiment of soldiers couldn't have persuaded them to put the bottle down. I stopped trying and focussed on what I could do; shield the little ones as best as I could. Comforting and distracting them from the regular outbursts of insanity. Protecting their childhood in the only way I could. Even becoming their Santa when Mam cancelled Christmas.

Mam always had to win every fight; she always had to have the last word. But not this Christmas Eve. For some reason she lost the fight to Dad. He responded to everything she said to him with another cutting remark. He simply wouldn't back down. The arguments went on and on, late into the night. I was listening from upstairs. When I looked at the clock, I saw it was past midnight, it was Christmas Day. Mam was screaming at Dad and for once he was calm and composed. I could hear Mam getting more and more agitated. Her voice increased a decibel every time she opened her mouth, Dad's voice remained at the same monotonous pitch. I could imagine him reading the *Chronicle*, deliberately winding her up. Then I heard an ornament flying across the room and smash into the wall.

'That's fucking it!' She screamed at the top of her voice.

Dad had won, which was a rarity.

I heard her running up the stairs. She came screaming into our bedrooms. 'That's it, fucking Christmas is cancelled because your dad is a bastard!'

She slammed our doors, then went to her own room. Bang! Another door slammed. I waited for fifteen minutes before I got up. I tiptoed to the door quietly, opened it and walked towards her bedroom door. I listened. I could hear her snoring gently. I opened the door. She was out for the count; she had passed out on top of the bed fully clothed.

I went downstairs. Dad sat nursing a bottle of Newcastle Brown Ale. He had a contented look on his face, which was more than unusual after one of their scraps.

I asked him if he was okay. He didn't answer me, he just looked into space, his head shaking slightly from side to side.

I walked back upstairs and about an hour later I heard him come up the stairs too, bouncing off the walls.

I was tired and weary but knew what I had to do. It was Christmas Eve and I knew that Santa wouldn't be paying us a visit anytime soon. My brother and sister would be up in a few hours looking for their presents and they would find nothing.

They can't do this to us, I thought.

I waited twenty minutes and looked in my parents' room. They were both unconscious. If a lightning bolt had struck their bedroom, they wouldn't have heard it.

I sneaked in and went into Mam's ottoman where she kept the presents every year. I carried them downstairs and placed them in their usual place.

Our Amy's little space was on the settee, our Stephen's on the chair and mine by the chair under the window. At least the kids would know Santa had been.

Christmas Day dawned, and the kids were excited. They tried to get me out of bed at about eight o'clock. I stayed where I was. Mam and Dad were still unconscious. I think they surfaced an hour or two later and joined in the festivities. They called up to me to open my presents. It was eleven o'clock and I still refused to get up.

Mam shouted up the stairs, 'You're spoiling our Christmas Day, you selfish bitch!'

I didn't care, it was my protest. It was me who had stayed awake most of the night to do their job.

And anyway, I'd had a sneaky look at my presents and sealed them back up. As usual, nothing I had asked for. Underwear again, fucking underwear! No toys, or a bike or a scooter, nothing I could play with. Mam got me some bangles I never wore and some flowery pyjamas I absolutely hated. As I opened the three small parcels, I wondered whether she even knew what I liked. I think she probably did but she didn't actually care.

I heard Dad's voice at the bottom of the stairs. 'Come on you lazy cunt, get up.'

I turned over and pulled the covers over my head. No, I'm not getting up, not yet anyway. Roll on Boxing Day.

We loved going to our dads' mother, our nana's, house on Boxing Day. We got lovely presents there. We would get slippers from Uncle Freddy and finally our feet would be warm again. We would also get a load of selection boxes and beautiful presents from Nana and Grandad, like jewellery boxes with dancing ballerinas. We got clothes that we actually liked, toiletries, sweets and chocolates wrapped in colourful Christmas paper. It seemed endless. We would catch up with our Aunts Melisa and Lynne, who were not much older than me because of a huge age gap from Nana having the boys. Nana would also put on a beautiful huge spread of food. The men, my dad, his brothers, Uncle Terry and Uncle Freddy and my grandad would all go to the local pub while Nana and Mam prepared the grand Boxing Day dinner and set the table. Nana would have been making homemade soup all morning, soup that had dumplings in. Mam was preparing turkey sandwiches with stuffing in, there were mince pies and lots of cake. Strawberry Gateau was my favourite and the Black Forest Gateau was beautiful and made us kids feel very special. It was exciting and a real treat like our Christmas Day should have been like. The excitement of these beautiful gifts and beautiful food was a real treat. The men were always late back. They would return all merry and singing and wishing everyone happy Christmas. Me and my sister hated that part though, receiving sloppy kisses with that stale smell of beer on their breaths.

Sometimes they would bring back a handful of people from the pub with them. The drink flowed and now Nana and Mam were joining in. At the start of the alcohol intake and festivities it was great fun. They were all in good spirits, not drunk, just merry. Then without fail someone, or perhaps more than one, would tip over the edge and the atmosphere would change.

This Boxing Day was slightly different. Everyone was merry and playing board games or sitting around the huge dining room table eating, drinking and having a good natter or sing song. In fact, I recall wondering when someone was going to kick off. It was surely long overdue? But no. It wasn't going to happen today. It was love and peace to all mankind, just like my teacher had said Christmas was all about.

I needed the toilet and when I tried the downstairs toilet it was busy. I skipped upstairs to the other toilet, which was right next door to Uncle Freddy's bedroom.

Whilst sitting on the toilet I heard giggling next door. People were whispering and I tried to hear what they were saying but couldn't quite make the words out. I didn't flush the toilet; I didn't want to make a noise. I tiptoed towards Uncle Freddy's bedroom and opened the door quietly; I just popped my head around. In sheer disbelief my jaw nearly dropped to the floor as I saw Mam lying on top of Uncle Freddy. They were giggling and kissing each other. I was around eleven at the time and, to be honest, I never once thought of the consequences of my actions, but I ran downstairs as fast as my legs could carry me because this was a great secret. To me it was like a huge exciting bit of gossip and I had discovered it. I burst into Nana's sitting room and just blurted out that Mam was kissing Uncle Freddy on his bed. For some reason I expected them to laugh as the atmosphere that day was all laughter. I don't know if I was trying to join in and be part of the fun, or if I was just immature for my age. I had no concept of the damage it would cause; it was just me, usually invisible, with news to share.

In hindsight, I should have said nothing and kept it in the file in my head with all the other secrets.

The house erupted. I was instantly stunned; I'm waiting for the laughter and what came instead was sheer fucking chaos.

Dad jumped up out of his chair along with Nana and Grandad.

They were trying to stop him getting out of the room.

'Wait there,' they shouted, 'the bairn has made a mistake!'

Dad was shouting and screaming. 'There's no fucking mistake, I know that slag.'

He was calling his brother a cunt at the top of his voice. Grandad had blocked the doorway with his body, Dad couldn't get past him.

Freddy and Mam had heard the commotion and came downstairs.

Freddy sheepishly poked his head around the doorframe. 'What the hell is up with him?'

Dad lunged straight at him and started throwing punches. Mam was screaming at Dad and Nana and Grandad were screaming at all of them. I covered my ears with my hands and the tears started to well up in my eyes.

Freddy was trying to explain that nothing had happened, but Dad kept lunging at him with punches as Freddy tried to stop him. Poor Grandad was in the middle pulling his sons apart, going ballistic with the pair of them. Dad was not letting it go though, he kept lunging with fists to the point that Uncle Terry was getting involved. They were all trying to keep Dad away from Freddy as he continued to protest his innocence.

We kids were just shocked at all the punching and screaming. Or rather my young aunts were, as clearly this wasn't the norm in their house. In our house it was commonplace but this time it was different it was in Nana's house and the fight the biggest ruckus I had ever seen. Terry was hitting Freddy and Freddy hitting Terry and Dad hitting both of them, sometimes at the same time while poor Grandad, trying to break it up, was probably getting hit by all three of them. And there was Mam right in the mix too, trying to hit Dad, accusing him of overreacting.

I cowered in the corner trying to make myself as small as possible wondering when some of them would start to hit me. I was left feeling incredibly guilty. On Boxing Day too, my favourite day of all days. Me…what was wrong with me, why did I do that, why had I even opened my mouth?

Poor Freddy had bought me the nicest slippers, the best slippers I had ever had, all warm and furry with little Christmas decorations on. Our parents were screaming at each other. Mam announced we were leaving.

'No,' I muttered to myself, 'not today. It's Boxing Day, the best day of the year.'

'We're fucking leaving,' Mam screamed. 'Get your fucking coat,' she said to me.

I was stunned but had the good sense to round up my presents; I sure as hell wasn't going to leave them behind. We walked out of the door. It was going to be a long, long night.

4

Jekyll & Hyde

That argument with Mam and Dad continued forever. Every time they were drunk it would resurface. They both took out their frustrations on me. Mam because I had stopped her, and Dad just for the hell of it, because it was me, and because I was a 'big-mouthed cunt'.

I carried the guilt and I learned to stay quiet. I was such a slow learner in many respects. It had been drummed into us kids that 'children should be seen and not heard.'

I now knew why.

We moved house again, this time to a place called Fawdon. Both sets of grandparents lived nearby, and our jazz band's stomping ground was just around the corner. I dared to believe that a degree of normality might be on the horizon and whenever there was trouble at our house, I could run away to one of my nanas and take the little ones with me.

It had been a house exchange and although the location was great for amenities, the house was in ruins. The walls were painted purple, it had no central heating and our kitchen cupboards were falling off the walls. At least we had some stability in the sense that we lived here until our young adult lives.

I give them their due, Mam and Dad both worked hard to clean up and redecorate the house. They fixed all the cupboards and everything that was broken. The walls were painted white, central heating was installed and new carpets were laid. When they were finished it looked lovely. We may have been poor and dysfunctional, but we weren't tramps and everything was spotless.

Mam was now working as an auxiliary nurse at the local mental institute, called St Nicholas and

Dad was still working for The Redifusion TV Company. But there was talk of uncertainty because of the Robert Maxwell scandal. I never knew what that meant, but it seemed serious enough.

They now frequented the St Nicholas Hospital club for staff members. The drinks were subsidised and cheap. It was the last thing Mam and Dad needed but they took full advantage of the cut-price alcohol and were there most nights. We hardly ever saw them, but I wasn't complaining. We had to endure a couple of hours of tension and animosity when we got home from school but we knew we wouldn't have to endure it too long. 99 times out of 100 it wouldn't be long before they took off, find their friends at the club and drown themselves in alcohol. At least we got some respite; we always tried to be fast asleep before they returned. The ritual door slamming often woke us up as the inevitable scrap broke out downstairs. We would lie awake until the early hours. We were sleep deprived and exhausted.

Mam was poorly every few months throughout our childhood,

she would take to her bed for days, sometimes even weeks, and we all took turns looking after her. She would bang on the floor and we would have to run to her room.

Dad says she was a drama queen and it was all in her head. It never stopped her drinking though.

Mam was now a Jekyll and Hyde character, very unstable, to say the least. Dad said she had always been unstable. I secretly agreed. One minute she would act reasonable, the next she would fling the dinner at you for no particular reason. One day I had the nerve to serve her mashed potato and gravy two days in a row, which saw the dinner and plate flying towards my head. I became quite adept at ducking out the way of a ceramic plate of hot pie and mash. No one ever knew the reason, and no one had the audacity to ask why she did what she did. We just washed the food off the walls and did as we were told.

Occasionally she emptied the entire freezer and binned everything, because we were a bunch of fucking pigs, she said. Nothing made sense; everything got swept under the carpet, no apologies, no reasoning, no explanations, no justifications. Nothing!

Another day she was curled up on the living room floor, her heart broken. When I asked why, she said she wanted a baby.

Huh! She couldn't look after us or herself, never mind a baby, how she ever worked in a mental hospital, and wasn't a patient, was beyond me.

Dad got made redundant and our lives were to become more unpredictable. Thanks very much Robert Maxwell. He had bought up Redifusion and then committed suicide by jumping off his boat, and everything went pear shaped.

Dad got depressed very quickly, being out of work. 'A man should never be out of work,' he would say.

He had been a hard worker, proud of the hours he would put in, and now the DSS had him signing on the dole with all the other 'layabout cunts'. He hated it. It dented his pride hugely. Every week he would be full of rage about the Job Club the dole made him attend. But that wasn't the worst aspect of 'the dole'. Dad did not have a wage coming in and funds were limited. It affected us all. There was no more evening reprieve as Dad was mostly at home drinking and not the social club.

We were now wearing hand me down clothes that didn't fit and looked tatty and torn.

The arguments increased, the violence increased, and the misery increased.

Every night one of us were sent to the 'offy' down at the corner shop to get Mam and Dad's beer in. It was initially four in four out, which meant four bottles of empty brown ale in, bringing four full bottles out. Then it was six in six out, before long it was eight in eight out. It just kept on increasing. They started to buy spirits too, but they bought their spirits themselves as the local shop owner would only give us kids the brown ale and the fags. (Not much regulation those days.)

You didn't have to be a genius to know that the little bit of money that was coming in was going on booze and cigarettes. There were no new school uniforms or new shoes and the weekly food shop took a hit too. I was told we were budgeting as Dad was on the dole now.

I got babysitting jobs and kept the money to save for my own clothes. Our Stephen would help neighbours and go to the shops for them and my sister walked every waif and stray that lived in the neighbourhood and pushed babies around in prams for 50p a time.

All the money we earned went on extra food or essentials with an occasional bar of chocolate or packet of sweets. Initially I thought it was great idea that I would get to keep the babysitting money to buy my own clothes. But I never realised how expensive clothes were and it took me forever to have enough for what I wanted, saving the odd 50p or £1.00 of what I earned. I was desperate for the new fashionable jumper dresses that had just come out. I got one eventually, but it had been out of fashion for at least a year by then. Still, I wore it, I had bought it, after all, and was so proud that I managed to do it without any help from my parents.

This was also the time when I went to high school and the kids would mock me for wearing a uniform that didn't fit. Mam and Dad said they couldn't afford the uniform. One of the neighbours' girls had got a new uniform and handed me her old one.

I told Mam, 'It doesn't fit.'

'It'll have to do,' she said.

The creases in my blazer were all in the wrong places and the kids laughed when I hung it over my school chair. The sleeves folded near the cuff because that's where her elbows had been. It looked as though my arms were still inside. However, the kids' tormenting was nothing compared to my parents' daily insults, so I laughed with them and at them. I could take anything my school friends threw at me. The insults at home were in a different fucking league.

'You're covered in spots, you look like a fucking pizza,' Dad would say. 'And that fucking brace your wearing makes you look like Metal Micky.'

He'd laugh. 'Thick, spotty and metal fucking teeth.'

My sister was called a fat cunt. He'd call her that several times a day. 'Fucking hell, that's all you do; eat, eat, eat. Your eyes are too big for your fucking fat belly.'

She would burst into tears and cry her eyes out. I would too, but I never let them see it, I'd wait until I was in my room.

Our brother was about seven when I was a teenager. He couldn't speak properly; me and Amy did his talking for him. I guess neglect and a lack of care or compassion didn't help with his speech, and the fact that every time he spoke, he was ridiculed or told to 'Shut the fuck up.'

He would grunt and hold out his hand and me and my sister knew he wanted a biscuit or food. Grunt and two arms outstretched meant he wanted comfort, a cuddle or a carry. Our parents were too distracted to notice his needs.

Dad just thought our brother was backward and would tell him that every day. I thought he was like the rest of us, emotionally stunted. I knew exactly what he was thinking: What is the point of learning to speak when I would soon get told to shut the fuck up.

Our vocabulary was extremely limited.

I just got on with it, sticks and stones and all that.

Me, my sister and brother often sat at the top of the stairs, listening to the fights downstairs. We made a hasty retreat when the fists started to fly, experience told us that if we stayed downstairs, we would inevitably get caught up in the melee.

The tension would build, and we would gather huddled together. It always escalated; there was no such thing as arbitration. As the ornaments started to fly and the 'fucks and bastards and cunts,' got louder and more aggressive, the two little ones would start to cry and beg for it to stop. I was running out of songs to sing to them.

We were a little older now, but it never became any easier listening to the violence downstairs. We lived in fear, but we had mastered hyper vigilance around the danger, although we still sometimes got it wrong and got caught out in an unprovoked attack.

Sometimes I didn't see it coming. Once morning, Dad was quiet, and nothing was out of place or anything. Then he came into the kitchen and barked, 'Make me a fucking cuppa.'

'I can't Dad, I'm late for school. I have to go.'

'I want a cuppa.'

'No,' I said with some defiance.

I was standing near the back door, trying to edge my way out, and he grabbed hold of me. He put his face in mine, he was so close that as he growled his spit hit my eyes. 'I want a fucking cup of tea you cunt, didn't you hear?'

He grabbed me by the shoulders and pushed me hard into the back door. I winced in pain as the towel handle attached to it dug into my back. I struggled to get my breath, gasping for air but he seemed not to notice, he just wanted his tea.

I was disobeying him, but I was beginning to get pissed off at my treatment. I'd had enough.

I took a sidestep to walk past him and once again he grabbed me and threw me into the back door. All I could think of was, don't you dare cry Karen. Again, I composed myself and took another step to the side. This infuriated him. How dare I defy him? He picked me up and threw me even harder into the back door.

He won, it hurt, and I cried. I cried because of the physical pain. I cried because I was powerless, but mostly I cried because I could never envisage this life ending.

'I'll make your tea Dad,' I said, wiping my tears.

I made his tea and I fucking hated him in that moment and I fucking hated my fucking life. How dare he do this, year in year out, was there no end to this torment?

'Good,' he said. 'Now I'm going to sit down and read my paper. You bring it through just as quick as you like.'

I nodded between the tears. I switched the kettle on as he walked through the door,

I made his tea. I peeked through the open door and saw him sitting behind the double sheet spread of his paper. I stirred in a spoonful sugar, cleared my throat, sucked in my cheeks and drew the biggest ball of spit I could muster into my mouth. I opened my mouth and let it drop into his cup. When I had exhausted every last bit, I stirred it in so that it could not be seen and took it in to him. My defiance had begun.

'There you go Dad,' I said as I handed it to him, 'I'm off to school.'

'Thanks,' he said, 'and don't be such a cunt next time.'

There's only one cunt in this house, I thought to myself as I left for school.

5

Escapism

The violence seemed to be escalating with age. Our parents now formed an alliance, took each other's side and ridiculed us more than ever before. We were thick, useless cunts; our parents hurled far more vicious and wicked insults at us than we ever heard in the playground. It was an endless world of punishment and abuse. Everything about us kids got on our parents' nerves. If we ate too loud, we were punished and even if we breathed too loud, we were slapped or punched, and God forbid if we cried. We were definitely not allowed to cry.

Our flagging self-esteems were on the floor. I could see my beautiful brother and sister fading before my eyes and there was nothing I could do about it. Our survival was based on staying out of the way and being invisible. If not, you would be attacked either by fists or Mam's slipper which really did leave their mark. It hurt way more than punches as the rubber sole stung our skin for hours.

We did our best to cope and we all had different coping mechanisms. My beloved books weren't working anymore. I simply couldn't concentrate on the words and couldn't ever make it to the end of a page. Besides, I longer believed in some stupid prince coming to rescue me.

My sister escaped the torment of our house by walking as many babies and dogs as she could and spent endless hours at these people's houses. Sometimes she never came home until Mam and Dad were unconscious in bed or comatose on the settee. My brother wagged school and then just didn't come home. God knows what he got up to, but he would go anywhere, and do anything, not to come home. My parents never even noticed he wasn't there.

I needed a new strategy, and to be fair, it was the 80's, so it wasn't hard to find.

Every night Dad would bark from over the top his *Evening Chronicle*, 'See this? See this fucking glue-sniffing lark, I'll kill you if you ever try this.'

I didn't know what he was talking about at first so when he left the room, I read his newspaper. There was a glue-sniffing epidemic in Newcastle, kids getting spaced out and not knowing where they were. What was it all about? *It must be good if there was an epidemic,* I thought to myself, the new craze to sweep the city according to the *Chronicle.*

He put the idea in my head himself. Seriously, it hadn't crossed my mind beforehand. *Might as well get hung for a lamb as sheep,* I thought. At least the beatings will be more tolerable if I'm spaced out.

And so it began. Our coping strategies and secret rebellions were about to shape our futures.

I couldn't wait to escape the madness. Mam was still coming

down with mystery illnesses every few months and was now taking to her bed more regularly, drinking on top of her medication and whispering in a breathless fashion like she was about to die. We were often summoned around her bed and informed of the new mystery illness. We become even more frightened than we were before. The doctor had told her not to take alcohol with her medication, but he might as well have been talking to a brick wall. Nearly every night she would vomit all over the place. The smell, Jesus I can still smell it now, brown ale vomit projecting out of her at an incredible force because of the four or five bottles she had downed. Sometimes I was covered in the stuff if I wasn't quick enough and of course it was my job to clean it all up.

Dad would leave her wherever she fell. 'You'll have to sit up with her,' he'd say.

I couldn't sit up all night with her; I was tired and needed to be up for school the next day. Dad didn't give a toss; he said she was a pig for drinking so much in the first place.

I would struggle to get Mam to bed and sit her up with a bucket rested between her chin and her chest. When I was sure she was settled I'd leave her and head to bed. Most mornings I would have a pool of brown sick to clean up before I left for school.

It was time. I needed some release.

'Please Denise, Dawn, please let's try it,' I begged my two school friends.

'No way, it's meant to be dangerous,' Denise said.

Denise was adamant she wasn't going to try it, but she looked the oldest and we needed her to go into the shop and buy it.

She hummed and hawed but eventually I talked her into it. We were terrified whilst waiting to see whether Denise would be served the much-awaited product or whether she'd be reported to the police. Tentatively we waited, and to my surprise she was served. Oh my God, she was given the glue. Result, I thought, excited to experiment with this taboo solvent. We were so naïve that we only bought a tube of Evo stick between the three of us, but it was enough to find out what all the fuss was about.

I seriously couldn't wait to get around the back of Kenton shops and try out this glue-sniffing lark that Dad had been talking about for weeks. We now had our 'stash' and we agreed to meet the next day after the end of classes.

I jumped out of bed the next morning, excited for the day ahead. All our plans had been arranged. After school we would meet up at the back of the shops and I would bring the carrier bags. Denise and Dawn were apprehensive; they had their own troubles at home too. None of us ever discussed much about what went on behind closed doors, but we knew we all had dysfunctions of varying degrees which made us firm friends.

Behind the shops there was a short cut and we sat down to try this new fad.

I poured some of the glue into the bag and started to inhale. I took a deep breath and the fumes stung and burnt the back of my throat. It was a horrible taste at first and I wasn't even sure if I was doing it right, but after the third inhalation I figured I must have been doing something right as I started to feel different.

I kept going, breathing and inhaling even harder as Dawn and Denise were now asking for their turn. It was working; Jesus Christ it was working and suddenly I didn't want to share this magic formula in a bag. It was an immediate getaway, a very quick way to leave this planet and be somewhere else where nothing mattered, and no one could hurt me. It made me feel warm and fluffy and in a bubble of safety. Like being cast in a movie, watching myself in space, or on some planet not known to man. But it made me feel powerful and directing my own narrative scene, rather than living in the brutal life directed by others. My body relaxed and my head for once was calm. I adored just watching the images and hallucinations of bright fluffy colours.

That's why they call it a trip, I thought to myself; it really is a trip away from the sad existence we lived in. It was cathartic; it gave me instant release from any confusing sad thoughts that floated round in my head. The trip seemed to last for hours and yet it was only half an hour or so, which was even better. I was in a vortex, where time didn't exist. It was another place and a better space to be. My friends were now impatiently crying out for their turn.

I knew I would definitely do this again. I immediately loved it. It was way better than waiting for any happy ending in a stupid book. I didn't want it to end but with three of us and only one tube, it didn't last long. I was coming down from the high, the epic feeling was fading, and I stood unsteadily on my feet with subtle, fluffy bits right at the end, until it gradually faded away. I was back in the real world and devastated to be back. Denise and Dawn didn't rate it as good as I did but they didn't have to escape the violence like me. Their world wasn't perfect, but they seemed to have the skill set to cope with their lives. Me? I was sick of coping, I now wanted total escapism. I loved every second of my trip, though I didn't like the taste it left in my mouth for hours after. The headache that followed wasn't good either, but overall, it was worth it, and I couldn't wait to do it again.

I wondered how I was going to get home without my parents suspecting what I had been up to.

From that moment on, glue-sniffing became my release, my friend, my parent, oblivion, all rolled into one. Trying to get hold of the substance was the only real difficulty.

Mam was now almost permanently ill. She was back and forth to the doctors and quieter than usual. She was still nasty, but it was different kind of nasty. We all had chores now, which was some relief to me as I didn't have to do everything, but we all had to step up to the plate.

There was added pressure on Dad too. He needed to get a job, and fast, as Mam was taking more and more time off work and there wasn't enough money for alcohol and cigarettes.

Even our school shoes had holes in the soles. We told our parents a few times that we needed new ones, but with money tight it fell on deaf ears. Besides, Dad said it wasn't essential, he would mend them instead.

Several days later Dad brought home a tin of Evo Stick to fix our shoes. He made carpet insoles and glued them inside. While Stephen and Amy watched in amazement as their little shoes were mended, I had one eye on the tin of Evo Stick. Dad didn't even put it away in a safe place, he left it by the kitchen door.

I immediately thought, *thank you God,* as it was the biggest tin of Evo Stick, I had ever seen. Every cloud has a silver lining and all that. I would take it and hide it the next time he was so intoxicated he couldn't string a sentence together.

I wouldn't have long to wait. He was pissed out of his brain that same night.

None of us took any problems to Mam, we just had to figure them out for ourselves or find out through other means. I had started my period and I was terrified to tell her. I knew she would be angry more than comforting, as now she would have to add sanitary products to the shopping list of the things we couldn't afford. *Fuck that,* I thought to myself and in the end, I asked a friend if she could get me something to use from her Mam. She gave me a handful of tampons. It was such a relief to use something more appropriate than toilet paper. A few days later I needed more and asked the same friend. She gave me some at break time but then made a point of telling just about every girl in school how she was keeping me in tampons. Oh God, I'd done it again. I'd brought shame to myself; I was the girl who couldn't afford a fucking tampon.

I made my mind up never to ask anyone for help ever again. I prepared for the inevitable awkward conversation with Mam. I was shitting myself.

There wasn't as much drama as I thought there would be, probably because she was sick in bed again.

'Fuck's sake, they're kept in the bathroom cabinet,' she said without too much fuss.

When Mam was poorly, she would speak very slowly and croaky. It was the same sound you make as you need to clear your throat with a cough to put it right. Well, her voice would do that, only she never coughed to put it right and she kept up that bloody croak for ages. It used to drive me mad. I would think, just cough for fuck's sake, and talk normally. But no, it was a pattern that would last for years and years. Same as her mystery illnesses.

'I need to see you all together, after school tonight,' Mam said one morning. 'I have some serious news to tell you all, so come home straight from school, it's important.'

'Wow, it sounds scary,' I said to my sister as we got on the bus for school. 'What do you think she is going to tell us?'

'I don't know, but I'm already scared,' Amy whispered.

'It will be fine man; with any luck she's leaving Dad or she's finally going to put us in a home.'

My poor sister cried even more. 'Don't say that.'

It was true. The thought of being put into a home was comforting. Esther Rantzen was always on the bloody telly saving all these kids. Being put into a home seemed to me to be a safer option than the way we were living. I'd often asked Mam if she would consider placing me in a children's home. She would laugh and tell her friends what I had said, and they'd all laugh. I was serious. I just thought it would be more structured and less violent and unpredictable. Perhaps I was naïve or living in a fantasy world, but I really did believe I'd have a better chance and that I'd get to meet Esther.

The curiosity of what Mam's announcement was going to be made it a very long day at school.

Finally, we gathered around Mam's bed that evening. She spoke to us in that croaky voice again, this time we listened though, without the irritation that it usually gave me.

'I have cancer kids, and it's not going to get any better. I'm really poorly and before I die, I'm probably going to end up in a wheelchair.'

Cancer. The only thing I knew about cancer was that it killed people. It was a scary word and meant the end was near. This scared us all very much. Our mam was not a nice mam, but the thought of her dying soon was really distressing. My brother was eight, my sister eleven and I was fourteen. We were speechless as we stood in shock at Mam's bed. Dad was out looking for work. I thought it was strange that she hadn't waited until he came in to make such a dramatic announcement. We started to cry, all three of us. Mam was too poorly to shed any tears. She closed her eyes breathing heavily; it was obviously to do with the cancer. She gave us no details other than what she had just said.

'How did you find out Mam?' Stephen asked.

'Cancer of what?' I asked. 'Is there a cure, couldn't you have treatment?'

Mam never replied.

'Shouldn't you be in hospital Mam?' Amy asked between her tears.

Mam's eyes remained closed.

So many questions with no answers or explanation, no details on what we should do, how could we help or when the inevitable would happen.

And then she suddenly said, 'Okay, let me rest now, you can all leave.'

We didn't know what to do or what to think or where to go, not that we ever did. At this age we all kind of went into ourselves more and on some level never really processed much. We didn't have any emotional skills as children, we weren't allowed any. We weren't allowed to get angry or sad or to ask questions. Our orders were to look pretty, smile and shut up, never ask for help, never reveal anything that goes on in the family to anyone outside.

Days passed and the atmosphere in the house was incredibly

quiet and sombre, like some big black cloud was looming. We couldn't escape from it. I guess we all wondered when Mam would die and what would happen to us afterwards. Lord only knows, Dad wouldn't be able to cope. Even as children we knew that.

Why had he not even mentioned it?

I told him what Mam had said. Every word.

He sat down at the kitchen table. He looked neither happy nor sad, he looked like he always did. 'Well, I'm not going to be pushing her around in any fucking wheelchair.'

It made sense now. All those times she vomited, her cancer was clearly in her stomach, I thought, and the beer just doesn't mix with her medication.

It was a mess; you would think she would try to stop drinking now that she had cancer. But no, if anything, she drank even more. I couldn't cope with the noise of the retching and the smell anymore, though I did stop wishing that she would choke on her own vomit as I had done in the past. After all, she was dying, and I wouldn't want to wish the choking on someone with cancer.

And then the guilt. Oh God, what had I done. It was me that made this happen with my thoughts and wishes and desires to get away from her. Now she was dying, and I felt terrible because it was my fault. God had listened to me for once. I will definitely go to hell for this.

I tried harder in the house and wrote poems for Mam and tried to be a better daughter. School went by in a bit of a blur and I used glue on my own to escape the feelings of fear and guilt.

Guess we just had to take it day by day.

6

Luck of the Irish

A few months later Mam was up and out of bed and going back to work with no explanation whatsoever, other than she was well now and didn't have cancer anymore. It was not to be spoken about again. So, we didn't mention it as we didn't want to jinx it. It had just gone; it was a simple as that. Another mystery.

I was relieved but also confused and a little pissed off that God could do a miracle like that on Mam and yet our lives were still perpetual abuse and turmoil, shit in every way you could imagine. It disturbed me somewhat, actually it disturbed me a lot. Surely, He could have sorted that out, it wouldn't have been half as difficult as curing our mam's cancer. Fucking typical, I thought.

Within days of Mam announcing she was 'cured,' normal service had resumed in the house and insanity, tension and dysfunction was back. It was strangely comforting. I guess you don't know how much you've missed the familiarity until it's gone. The abnormal had become our normal and without the adrenalin of constantly being on high alert there was just a numbness. It was unnatural. The usual mayhem was reassuring in the worst way imaginable.

Mam was taking too long reading the *Chronicle* one night, so Dad set fire to it. She didn't really notice until the flames really took hold. She was livid and hit the roof in a very healthy fashion, considering she had not long ago been dying. Me and my sister went to hide our giggles in the bedroom.

Dad had got himself a job as a kitchen porter at the hospital where Mam worked. I would pray that the staff noticed their mental health and would commit them both, but I've never had much luck. It was more of a strenuous job, so it took its toll on Dad. He was now getting so drunk after working long shifts at the hospital that it was easy to pinch a cigarette from his box, light it with his lighter and sneak it up to the bedroom. He was also doing a lot of sleepwalking. Mam said it was down to tiredness and anxiety. We would be fast asleep and at around 4am he would barge into our bedrooms and more often than not piss all over Amy as she was the nearest to the door. Sometimes he would open our wardrobe doors and piss in there too, other times he would be asking where his hospital kitchen trollies were. You never knew what was going to happen next. We used to hide under our quilts and hold them down so tight so we wouldn't get punched, pissed on or hit with something.

My friend Dawn was sleeping over one night, which was a rarity as Dad was so unpredictable, but this night our parents were going to some party, so I was allowed a friend to sleep. I forgot to mention that Dad sometimes sleepwalked and true to form, in he came at some ungodly hour.

His eyes were open, but he was clearly out of it. 'Where's me trolley?' he asked.

Dawn was genuinely scared.

I whispered, 'Don't worry, Dad's just looking for his kitchen trolley.'

She looked at him as he peered in the wardrobe. 'You mean he's off his fucking trolley.'

She wasn't far wrong.

I had started doing bits and bobs with hair and wanted to go to college when I left school to become a hairdresser. Friends were asking if I could dye their hair, or cut it, and considering I had never been trained I found it came naturally and I enjoyed doing it.

One day Barbara, a friend, came around for the classic wedge haircut. She had shoulder length hair and I had just completed one side of it. Dad was home early from work and I knew he wouldn't be too happy that Barbara was in the kitchen, but he knew I was training myself to get ready for leaving school, so he accepted it. Grudgingly.

He looked at her and nodded his head. 'Don't be long,' and then he walked out.

I was just starting to cut the other side of her hair when I noticed she was going quite pale. She turned very white and very quiet, then a strange shade of grey and then fainted, falling forward straight into our cooker headfirst. What a racket. Jesus Christ, she's dead, I thought as she bounced off the cooker and fell onto the floor motionless, a trickle of blood oozed from the side of her brow.

Dad came storming into the kitchen and went ballistic. He stepped over her. 'For fuck's sake look at the oven door.'

I looked. There was a large dent where poor Barbara head had butted the top of the oven door.

'It's your fucking fault for giving her too much coffee, you useless cunt.'

I was panicking. Poor Barbara was still lying on our kitchen floor and Dad was more concerned about the oven. I didn't know who to console first, Barbara or Dad. When she eventually came round,

Dad was swearing and cursing and threatening to send her a bill for what she'd done to the oven. I opened the back door so that she could get some air and poured her a glass of water. I cleaned up the blood and eventually Dad stormed out. Surprisingly, she didn't want her hair finishing, which was not going to be good for business. I think her ordeal had shocked her into a hasty exit, but I'm sure she inspired The Human League with the lop-sided haircuts as it honestly took off after that.

She ran very quickly down the path and never returned to have her hair cut.

The only regular visitors now were Amy's snotty-nosed kids from the street. After school Amy would go knocking on doors, asking people if she could push their children around in their prams for either money or conversation. Let's be honest, the dialogue was on the same level as in our house. These were some of the most deprived kids on the estate and she'd bring them back to our house. Our estate had an abundance of dysfunctional families and deprived kids. One set of parents over the road couldn't even tie their shoelaces together so they wore Velcro. They lived in joggers and T shirts which read, *Frankie Says Relax.*

They took the words literally as they did fuck-all, day in day out. My sister would ask to push their baby around and they'd hand her a family of kids as well as the Jack Russell. Overjoyed for the peace that was coming their way, they'd quickly close the door behind them. Amy, who was now in her element, walked the streets for hours with a kid either side of her, one in a buggy and a dog with the lead tied to her arm. She brought every childhood illness you could think of to our family.

Every now and then we would get a visit from our aunt who lived in Dublin. She was nothing like our mam. She was dripping in gold, wore expensive-looking clothes and had a nurturing, caring side to her. You could see why Mam was a little envious of her sister and she liked to tell us that Grandad Bert had favoured our aunt over her.

She had a touch of class, our aunt, and everyone wished to see her when she was visiting. She would sing songs, bake and asked questions and genuinely cared about how we were. Not that we could tell her the truth. The retribution wasn't worth it.

We would have fun when she visited. Everyone was in high spirits and we'd get to stay up longer, just staring in awe of her, especially when she sang. They'd all go to the local together, then bring back people from the pub. The men loved her; she was like a magnet to them. These visits would be once or twice a year throughout our childhood, but eventually alcohol even ruined that.

One night everyone had been having a merry time, all the family had been around to visit our aunt. Then it was just her and Mam left, drinking whiskey and vodka. At some point, long into the night, I woke up to screaming and fighting and quickly realised the two sisters were going hell for leather at each other. They were like wild cats, I had never heard anything like it, but there was nothing I could do. Dad was passed out in bed, thank God; he didn't hear a thing. Amongst the screaming, crying, punching, slapping and scratching were the sounds of our house getting smashed up again. I tried to piece together why they were screaming at each other. Apparently, Mam had said that she thought my brother was not Dad's, but our aunt's late husband Derek's. She supposedly had an affair with him back in the day. This understandably had enraged my aunt. By now you never knew if what Mam said was truth or fantasy, or plain attention-seeking. I was shocked that someone would reveal such a tale, especially to their own sister. I lay awake wondering if my brother was my stepbrother, then remembered he has the same chin as the rest of us. A Kirk Douglas chin, besides, he was as thick as me, so he must have been my real brother. Alcohol though, huh?

The next day they were very quiet and I'm not even sure if they remembered why they were fighting in the first place.

Neither Dad or anyone else got to hear what was said and, thank God, this one was swept swiftly under the carpet, but every now and then it would make me wonder.

I was definitely going to college; I had applied as soon as I had left school and I had been accepted. I was excited, this was a new chapter in my life, and I couldn't wait. Boys still didn't interest me as I was socially awkward and didn't feel good enough about myself. But hairdressing I could do, and I was good at it. I was told by the college tutor that I would have to pay two hundred pounds to fund the kit I needed. I was worried, how would my parents feel about paying that? After all, two hundred pounds could buy an awful lot of alcohol.

It was a lot of money back then but in the grand scheme of things it was nothing extortionate because it covered the cost for the two years' training. I approached my parents, said that I could do hair at home and pay them back. To my amazement they actually agreed that it was a good idea.

Wow, I thought, I'm growing up and life is getting better. This was real communication.

I was sixteen and experimenting with my own hair. I never really knew my identity so it would change frequently, like my personality. Like a chameleon I constantly morphed to try and fit in with my surroundings. One day I liked David Bowie the next it was Duran Duran. It all depended on who I was hanging around with.

By time I got to college I realised that the girls in my class were a lot more mature than me, so I adapted to fit in with humour and tried to make them laugh. It worked. I loved this process and part of my life. I worked hard and thrived in the salon atmosphere. I struggled with the theory but was a natural at the practical side. I even won a competition for best and most original haircut at the end of the term and my drawings and photos were proudly hanging on the college walls. It felt surreal.

My parents never came to any of the college events. Hell, they hadn't ever attended any parents' evenings at school, no school plays, summer fete's, or sports days. It was nothing new, but I was starting to notice how other parents were interacting with their children and families and it sure was nothing like ours. Still, what you've never had, you've never missed. Besides I had a family of friends now and I didn't need the negativity. I had praise for good work and recognition for my achievements. The more recognition I received for good work, the harder I would work. I liked it. I liked it a lot.

In the 2nd year we were to be sent on placements at real salons in the Newcastle area and although I dreamed of working on a cruise ship and travelling the world, my low self-esteem prevented me from ever trying to get into these lucrative and luxury salons. I told myself I simply wasn't good enough. I'd pass Steiner (the salon that trained their staff to a high standard, to board and work on the cruises) every day, knowing it was where I'd have to go to finish my training. But every day on the Number 30 bus, I'd stare in through the window and it just looked so professional that I could never bring myself to apply for a position there. I was terrified of rejection and failure and working in a high-end shop, to me, meant that people would see my failings and inadequacies. I knew that I wouldn't be able to take the criticism. To me when somebody criticised me it meant I was useless. A useless cunt, as my father used to say.

So, I took the easy route. I took placements in little nana shops up the West End of Newcastle, because that way I could be the best and shine and get the praise that I so desperately needed for my flagging esteem. It was safer, less risky and the clientele was easier to please.

I became the most modern hairdresser in those tiny dingy places. It wasn't hard, I would work my way up, it was achievable, and I let my ambitions fade.

Mam and Dad were a lot more settled as time went by. They were probably a little too old to be knocking lumps out of each other, but

I think they also accepted they were going to stay together, no matter what. They still fought and had scraps, but it wasn't as vicious as it had been. However, they joined forces on ridiculing us and you still had to occasionally duck to miss a dinner plate or a punch in the head.

Mam got sick again.

It wasn't long after my Dad's dad, my Grandad had died. Again, we were asked to meet around her bed at a certain time so that we would all be together.

Our immediate thought was her cancer was back, so we were already apprehensive.

Mam had her croaky voice back and she started talking really slow. 'I'm needing a hysterectomy; I may have cancer of the womb. It's a massive operation and I will be bedridden, possibly for months. It's nothing to worry about but it is a huge operation so I'm going to need you all to help me through it, okay?'

'Of course, we will help Mam,' we said collectively.

'Are you really going to be okay Mam?' I asked.

She looked at me sadly and croaked, 'Yes, though it is a very dangerous operation and the anaesthetic could kill me.'

Jesus fucking Christ.

'But it needs to be done, otherwise I will almost certainly die.'

My sister burst out crying. I looked over to her and my first thought was that she was going to need better beta-blockers than the ones she was using. Me and my brother just looked at each other, worry etched into our faces.

'When have you got to get the operation?' Stephen asked.

'Is there anything we can do to help?' I said.

'Just let me rest. I'll not know when the surgery is until I get a letter from the hospital.'

It was worrying for several reasons. Firstly, I didn't know if my little sister could take much more of this, her panic attacks were back, and she was constantly afraid and nervous. She would jump at any sound and never slept well. Also, we were all still grieving for our grandad, it was still incredibly raw. How would Dad handle it if Mam died too?

The thought of Mam possibly dying in surgery frightened the life out of me and even if she did survive, she would be bedridden for months. I'd have to look after her and do everything.

I was already falling asleep on the bus most mornings because I was so tired. My exams were coming up and the study on top of all the housework and looking after my brother, sister and my dad was taking its toll. Jesus, is this really what life will always be like?

It was one problem after another. We didn't have Google in those days but next day I was going to ask my biology tutor all about it as soon as I got to college. The lecturer would surely explain how my mam got cancer and what would happen during a hysterectomy. What and why and if's and but's may finally be answered. Our parents couldn't or wouldn't explain and understanding it all at least helped with the fear of the unknown.

Dad never mentioned a thing. He was quiet and withdrew into himself. He put down for extra hours at the hospital and worked overtime.

I still occasionally used the glue to block things out, but not on a regular basis and now always on my own. I just liked to shut the world out for a few hours and embrace the high that came with the fumes. The beautiful colours and cotton wool feelings that came with it were too good to give up, but I was aware that it wasn't socially acceptable. A glue bag stuck to your face on the way home from college is never a good look. I kept it quiet and just used occasionally when I needed a release.

The days rolled into weeks and the weeks rolled into months and still there was no letter from the hospital. And like the last time, she started to recover again and there was no mention of the hysterectomy or cancer.

This woman has nine fucking lives, I thought to myself, but it was a relief to just get back to being normal again and not have to worry about her dying. She was back out of bed and back at work, though Dad kept up the over time.

He now worked every Christmas Day too. He said it was fairer for the young'uns to have the time off with their kids. We were older now. He didn't need to be home. My brother was only ten and my sister thirteen, still kids. I couldn't understand it but at least there were no dramas.

Everyone was busy for a time and we passed each other only occasionally. We all seemed to have our own separate lives, our own agendas. Mam had gone on to night shifts and I was mostly at the salon because they had kept me on once I graduated from college.

Life was peaceful to a point.

And yet there was always something that would upset the daily rhythm. Mam slept most of the day but kept getting woken up with people knocking on the door; cold callers trying to sell anything from vacuum cleaners to cosmetics. She pinned a massive notice to the front door.

Do not disturb, I work night shifts.

The cold callers still knocked. More fool them, I thought, as we all knew Mam had a vicious temper, but it was even worse if she had been woken up on nights.

I was coming in one lunchtime. It was bedlam.

She had a salesman by the throat, 'Can't you fucking read?'

She was dressed in her nightie, hair all over the place. Her hand was balled in a fist and she held it up level with the man's head. She was pointing at the notice. 'What fucking part can't you read, you blind twat?'

He managed to wriggle free and ran up the path. Within seconds he had disappeared. Another neighbour two doors down was standing outside her door, staring open-mouthed.

'And what the fuck are you looking at?' Mam bellowed at her.

The neighbours must have thought we were nuts when I think of it now. Mam fought a lot with them. She never backed down no matter who they were and how many there were. Once Mam was finished with them, they rarely darkened our doorstep again.

7

My Friend Vodka

I was approaching my eighteenth birthday and the family said they were going to have a party for me.

'Me...really?'

It was my first ever party, I was surprised and incredibly excited. My parents really were changing, and I felt it was because I was becoming an adult.

The party was to be held at the local pub and all the family would be there. All the girls from college and the girls I worked with at the salon were coming too. I honestly couldn't wait to officially become a *bona fide* adult, all legal and grown up.

The day the party came I walked into the pub with a couple of my college friends and it was packed with people. They all turned to face me as I walked in. They were there for me; it was quite alien to me. I was overwhelmed and felt really awkward. I wasn't used to this attention, positive attention at least. Everyone was asking me what I wanted to drink, and I didn't know what to have. My friend said try a vodka and coke, you'll like it.

The vodka and coke came in a small glass with a stem to hold and a cherry in it. I instantly loved how it looked in my hand, I felt like a grown up and it looked sophisticated. I took my first sip and immediately fell in love with the taste, then I felt the warmth deep inside me. I was on cloud nine. I drank it quite fast and the second one was waiting for me on the bar. Again, I picked it up, admiring the glass and relishing the taste, but adoring the effect even more. I caught a glimpse in the bar room mirror and for the first time in my life, I liked what I saw.

I was instantly sociable, no fear and I felt confident. Boys were attracted to me and talking to me and I couldn't believe how fantastic I felt. I suddenly understood it. I got why my parents adored this fucking alcohol stuff. I loved that it was socially acceptable, and I didn't have to hide my shame in a C&A carrier bag to feel good. I loved how it transformed how I felt about myself and other people. Suddenly everyone was a friend and not a threat. We danced, we sang, we loosened up. I was having conversations with my parents. This was a first, real lengthy conversations that we had never ever had before, ever. Even the ugly guys that I went to school with now looked like Don Johnston. What was in this stuff? Every time I went to the toilet and saw myself in the mirror, I felt more attractive. I looked taller, more mature I was even getting long lingering birthday kisses off some of the boys. Well, at least up until I saw my dad glare over at me.

It suddenly dawned on me that alcohol wasn't the problem. Alcohol was the solution.

And, dear God, what a wonderful solution I had found. I'd had the best night of my entire life, that night of 28 December 1985. I had found my best friend, my new lover, my voice, my counsellor, my esteem. It was my everything, and I adored it.

I ended up chasing that very night for the rest of my life.

Alcohol was everything I wanted. It was the answer to my eighteen years' of prayers, it was my personality in a jar that brought me alive. It took away all my insecurities and fears, my inadequacies and it loved me back. It made me strong and courageous, it made me feel attractive and wanted. It felt like the parent I never had, the lover I dreamed of, the solution to life's woes. It had everything I needed. It was most definitely medicinal, and I wanted more.

My love affair with it had started and I couldn't wait until the following Saturday to go down the Big Market in Newcastle, the place I had heard so much about.

I got the usual warnings from people saying to stay safe and the Big Market could be dangerous at times. But I felt invincible, what the fuck was going to happen to me? I had lived in a warzone my entire life, what could be worse than that? I just needed a reliable friend who enjoyed this stuff as much as me and who was also raring to go.

I found Lola. She lived close by and was also a hairdresser and wanted to be down 'the Toon' as much as me.

We arranged our first night out and she said she would come to mine to get dressed and bring a bottle with her. Not that I thought we needed a bottle beforehand, wasn't the excitement of reaching the destination and ordering our medicine enough? But funnily enough, as the day went on, I got butterflies with excitement and a touch of fear. Bringing a bottle along while we got ready made sense. God, why did everyone else seem to have the answers long before me?

Lola knew it all. Where we were going, how much we would need and what we should wear (this was going to be difficult). I'd never really followed fashion and it was only recently that I was making a wage, but I had little idea what to wear for such occasions. Lola kept me right.

I pulled something out of my wardrobe.

'No, you can't wear that,' she said, 'it's so dated, let's see what you've got.'

She opened my wardrobe and we were sipping our Cherry B mixed with Babycham because apparently it got you drunk faster. Placebo effect, who knows?

She gasped.

'Is this all you've got?' she asked.

Embarrassed, I said, 'Yes.'

I was only recently learning about how to apply makeup and style my hair, which perfumes were fashionable and what kind of things I should be wearing for my age.

'You're going to have to go shopping Karen,' she said. 'But for now, try on this with that.'

She hurled a couple of items at me that I would never have thought would have matched, but she was cool and stylish, so I did what I was told.

I was a late starter, for sure, but was ready for a crash course in enjoying being a young adult.

Mam was on the settee as I was leaving.

'What do you think?' I asked,

I don't even think she looked up from the paper, she just hmm'd me out the door.

We were dressed, tipsy and ready to go down the Big Market. I couldn't wait.

The Big Market was jumping. I had never even come close imagining it to look the way it did. Bar after bar after bar, men, handsome and well-dressed men, all over the place. There were girls dressed in miniskirts and high heels no matter what the weather, and music bouncing on every corner. I was fascinated. Our first port of call was City Vaults. The place smelt of vomit and your shoes stuck to the carpet, wall to wall full of people spilling their drinks all over the place, but you got three shots of vodka and coke for £1.

Lola knew the ropes. I couldn't believe how crushed it felt and how you had to wrestle to get served at the bar. It was magical. You couldn't really talk, but you didn't really want to. I soaked up the atmosphere in this new world like sand swallows water. Everyone was happy and either dancing, kissing strangers or just trying to stand steady on their feet. It was January and freezing, but most were a bare armed, in tight t-shirts and skimpy dresses, not feeling the cold at all. We skipped and staggered from bar to bar, had a couple of drinks, then on to the next one, and the next and then the next.

If you hadn't copped off and had a kiss with at least one guy you'd failed. I didn't know if this was just a Newcastle thing or if it was just us. But it was standard and those were the rules. If you remembered the guy's name, the next day then you were a genius. If a guy asked for your number, you'd tell him your number but change the last digit, never to been seen again. If you got it wrong someone else would have to step in. I got it wrong a few times and gave my real number out and would get my sister to say they had the wrong the number.

She played the role well, 'I'm only fifteen and definitely was not down the town last night.'

As she hung up, we collapsed into fits of laughter.

God, these were good times. We had such amazing nights and laughed until our bellies were sore. But the night seemed to end way too soon for my liking. I always wanted more.

We did this every weekend but turning up back home at 11.30 at night was starting to annoy my parents. I tried to be as quiet as possible and put my key in the door and go straight upstairs to bed. But many times, Mam and Dad were still downstairs drinking themselves and getting all lairy and looking aggressive. They were spoiling for a scrap.

I'd pop my head around the living room door and slur, 'I'm just going straight to bed, night, night.'

Then I'd try to get away.

'You been out looking like that?' Dad would say

'Oh, shut up and don't start man, for God's sake,' Mam would say

'But have you seen what she's wearing? Look at her hair man, I mean, what the fuck do you call that?'

'It's the fashion, they're all doing it.'

My God, Mam was actually sticking up for me. That was a first.

'Sheba, watch her,' Dad ordered.

'Ah, for fucks sake, I'm not playing this game. I'm going to bed Dad.'

'Don't you ever swear in this house!'

Boom! He was up on his feet with his fist up to my face snarling, 'You ever swear in this house again and I will burst your fucking lips, you hear me.'

'Yes Dad,' I turned and started walking up to bed.

'You fucking hear me you useless cunt?'

'Yes Dad, I'm sorry.'

And I'd walk up those stairs thinking, you fucking bullying arsehole. I hate you.

Sometimes I'd get brave and whisper it and I'd hear him say. 'What did you say, what the fuck did you say?'

'Nothing Dad, I need to sleep.'

I would hear him say to Mam as I climbed the stairs, 'What did she say, what the fuck did she say?'

I'd go to bed and swear to God that when I had a family, I would never, ever treat them like that. Ever.

8

Walk of Shame

My brother was now twelve, my sister fifteen and me eighteen. My sister, out of fear, just hung on Mam's every word now, which Mam loved. But it came at a heavy price. My sister would pay that price for years to come. My brother was now getting a lot of the verbal and physical abuse, mostly from Dad.

I was very rarely there because of work and my regular weekends out, but my brother was now bringing trouble to the door regularly. He was fighting a lot and the *Wagger Man* came to the house as he missed school at least four or five days every month.

He was also into cannabis, his new escape. Mam and Dad were having a sing song one night, laughing together with their arms around each other. Behind their backs my brother grew pale and grey, started swaying and then gagged and retched. He was having a whitey due to the cannabis. Dad would occasionally look around to see where our Stephen was and me and my sister would distract him, saying 'Sing it again, sing it again Dad!' just to keep him facing us. The cannabis hadn't agreed with Stephen, but our parents were so drunk they couldn't tell, and our distracting gave him enough time to slip out the back door to vomit. My sister and I found it hilarious, especially as our parents thought we were laughing with them. We weren't, we were creased at our poor brother and the effects of his joint. Teamwork that night saved our brother a good beating.

The more I went out at the weekends, the more I decided to not come home. It just wasn't worth the hassle. I'd crash at Lola's place but occasionally if we had scored or we had lost each other in the Big Market, then I'd have no choice to but to crash at some stranger's place.

I had no sense of the consequences; all I knew was that kipping at a stranger's place was safer than going home. And if they could supply more alcohol then I was happy. It wasn't great for my moral compass though, as I quickly found out. I'd come to and not know where the hell I was or who I was with. Worse still, I didn't know how the hell I was going to get home.

I tried the usual, sneak out the door and leave a fake number on the side, or sometimes I just had to pluck up the courage to wake the person up and ask what the address was, so I could order a taxi. Sometimes I had to ask for the fucking taxi fare. Oh, the shame.

I never knew who was more shocked, me or the stranger.

'Excuse me, where am I, nice to meet you. I need an address for the taxi?'

As I slipped out the door I'd shout, 'Call me', praying I'd never see the person ever again, no matter how nice he was.

Oh God, the walk of shame the next day, trying to piece the night together and knowing I was still in last night's party clothes on a Sunday morning. It was never a good look. I'd turn my key in the door as quietly as I could and go straight to bed not to be seen until early afternoon.

I'd bide my time, wait until no one was in and ring Lola to find out how the night had been. I'd ask her to fill in the gaps of my missing jigsaw, who the boy was or how many drinks we'd consumed.

Even from the start, there were differences. Once I started to drink, I didn't want to stop. Lola knew when it was time to go home, I never wanted to go home. Also, she didn't have missing parts of the night, I always did. Wherever she landed she kept quiet, never divulging much and never seemed to have any shame about it. Bloody hell, I did, buckets of it. Guilt, shame and remorse. I'd sit and stew all week, assure myself that I would never drink as much again, only to repeat the same thing the following Saturday.

Around about April, me and Lola were doing our rounds downtown and dancing away when I spotted one of the lads that I used to go to school with. I'd had a crush on him for a couple of years and we started talking, but his annoying little friend took over the entire conversation.

'Introduce me then,' he kept saying to Paul. 'Introduce me, man.'

He was very loud and in your face. To be honest, he scared me a little. He was too abrupt for my liking and wouldn't take no for an answer. He was forceful and arrogant, pulling out wedges of cash and showing off. I wanted him to go, but he wasn't having it and by now I could see Paul was slightly intimated by this very loud character. He backed away. That devastated me. I'd fancied Paul for a while now and this guy was spoiling it. He drove me mad with questions, where were we going next, where were we going for last orders, where I lived, what I did for work, could he have my number? Persistent fucker I thought, *Howay Lola, we got to go now.*

'Who was that?' Lola asked.

'Apparently his name is Tommy and he works with Paul. But he's scary, so let's disappear.'

We left and I was genuinely gutted that I couldn't get to talk to

Paul properly. This bloody Tommy had spoilt my night but not to worry; alcohol would make it good again. My best friend alcohol.

It was Monday teatime and I was in my room, where I practically lived, listening to Diana Ross and The Supremes. I heard someone shouting and turned down the music. It was Mam, shouting at the bottom of the stairs. 'Karen if you turn that bloody music down you will hear what I'm trying to say to you.'

'What?' I said.

'There's a lad at the door and he won't go away.'

Confused I came down the stairs and was gobsmacked.

In the loudest voice possible like a proper Del Boy there was Tommy. 'I've come for a haircut,' he grinned.

Oh My God, he knows where I live, I thought to myself. *How, why?*

I've never been that assertive, people-pleasing has always been a weakness of mine and I'd rather avoid any type of uncomfortable feelings and conflict, if possible. I had never been taught boundaries. Without the alcohol I was shy and awkward Karen again. I had no idea how I was going to get out of this as I had nowhere to run.

He obviously sensed my anxiety and discomfort and said, 'Look, I'll just have a haircut, I've heard you're good and then I'll leave you alone, alreet.'

I couldn't say no, so in he came to get a haircut. It was the quickest cut I had ever given to a customer. He paid me something ridiculous like £20.00 which was a hell of a lot in those days, a normal haircut was about four quid. He refused to go until I gave him a kiss. I found my voice this time and was saying no.

'Okay then, just kiss me here on the cheek,' he said, 'and like Van Goff I'll be off.'

Had he really just said that? Oh my God, who is this bloke?

But as I was desperate to get rid of him, I leaned forward and went to kiss his cheek. He then turned sharply so my lips touched his and he burst out laughing.

'See, I knew you wanted to. Cheers for the haircut.'

As he left, he banged on the living room door and peered in. 'Thanks very much Mr and Mrs Slater.'

They were stunned but I think they liked his cheek. I didn't and now he knew where I lived.

I popped my head around the living room door and immediately apologised. They looked happy.

'Have you seen what he pulled up in?' Dad said.

I looked out the window and expected to see a flash car like a sports car or BMW. Mortified, I saw a giant-sized lorry with his name painted all over it, parked in the street so that the neighbours couldn't get by. Oh my God, I thought.

'He seems alright, him like,' Mam said.

'Owns his own business too, by the look of it,' Dad said.

I didn't care, he still scared the shit out of me. I went to hoover my room.

Life was pretty good. I had a good job, worked hard and earned a decent wage. I'd also go to people's houses after work to cut hair. I was out every Saturday and now sometimes Sundays. I had a wardrobe of fashionable clothes. Lola might have disagreed with that statement, but I was slowly finding myself.

Mam and Dad were even having a spell of normality. Mam hadn't been sick for a few months now and it was all doable, I was coping. It wasn't the life I'd dreamt of, but it had improved considerably which was a good sign. I loved growing my little business with my own clientele and it was getting busy. I had plenty spare cash. Life was looking up.

It was a Tuesday afternoon and I was at work cutting a client's hair when the florist man turned up with a gigantic bouquet of flowers.

Fran, the boss, said, 'Wow! Look at the size of them, who's it for?'

I honestly never for a second thought they were for me and carried on cutting my clients hair. Then I heard the lasses giggling and saying, 'Karen, they're for you.'

My client looked at me and told me to have a look. I put my

scissors down and could feel my face going red as I walked across the salon floor and nervously picked up the little card that was addressed to me. I opened it.

'Well?' everyone was saying.

I read the scribble.

Can't wait to see you again, Tommy. XXX

'Oh, Christ. Aren't they beautiful?' everyone was saying. 'It's the biggest bouquet I've ever seen', someone else said.

Gill took the card off me and read it. 'So, who is this Tommy?'

Just then the phone rang, and Fran answered it. 'Karen it's your mam.'

I mouthed over to my client, 'I'm sorry, I won't be long.'

'No bother pet, you're popular today, aren't you?'

'Hello Mam, sorry I have a client, what's up?'

I could hear the excitement in her voice. 'Er, well pet, you'll never guess what? The biggest bunch of pink carnations have just arrived at the door for you from that Tommy lad.'

Shit, shit, shit.

'You'd be silly not to get to know him. He's brought us a huge box of fruit and veg and chocolates too. I've given him our number and he will ring you tonight. What a lovely lad he is.'

I could almost see the pound signs flashing in my parents' eyes. *Shit! What have I got myself into?* I thought as I put down the phone and went back to finish the poor woman's hair.

I hadn't even kissed him, never dated him. What was he playing at?

I know I should have felt flattered, but I didn't. I felt scared. I also knew everyone around me was rooting for me to at least date this guy and see how it went. They were talking about his business and how he was so successful at such a young age. They said he must be crazy about me.

But that was the thing, nothing had happened between us. There was something very controlling right from the start, only I don't suppose I recognised it then, or did I? I was so used to burying my head in the sand. It sure as hell made life more bearable when you see the good in even the not so good. This guy would not take no for an answer and my self-esteem was so low that all these gifts mounting up made me feel obliged to at least go on a date with him.

The abuse from my parents temporarily stopped, the coercive control from my first ever boyfriend was about to begin.

The phone rang and Tommy said,' I'm not taking no for an answer, l will pick you up at 7pm. Be ready.'

My intuition was screaming no, but I meekly agreed.

9

Dysfunctional Attraction

So, I finally had a boyfriend. I was a late starter and wished I'd never started, to be fair, because me and romance did not seem to go together. It was nothing like those books I used to read or the movies where two people fall in love and the man has rescued the damsel in distress and they live happily ever after. Oh God, no. If you grow up in a dysfunctional home, you're going to attract, or be attracted to, dysfunctional people. Only, at eighteen you don't know any of this and you just plod on, wearing rose-tinted glasses and disregarding any red flags that appear on the horizon.

Tommy was manipulating and controlling from the start although we didn't recognize that at the time. It was easy enough to convince my parents he was the guy for me by bringing them a huge box of fruit and veg every week and buying my siblings carrier bags full of sweets. Oh, he played the part well and they were all taken in as he showered gifts on them. He could simply do no wrong.

Tommy knew everyone and everyone knew Tommy. He had a presence about him, he was unapologetic and demanded you see and hear him wherever he went. He knew every villain in Newcastle and portrayed an air of confidence and assurance, with a bit of cockiness and arrogance at the same time. And dare I say, he was a closet misogynist.

He introduced me to some of the main villains in the city. I was on edge; I could sense that these men were not to be messed with. It was a dangerous game and you learned quick to not ask questions or look at any of them twice as this meant you were flirting, and like a dog, you've already been pissed on and claimed.

You didn't get to say no to Tommy, you were meant to look pretty on his arm, not have an opinion and prioritise a man's needs first. A man's man some would say. It was flattering at times, as he was one step ahead opening doors and pulling out chairs. 'A real gentleman,' some of the old folk would say. He'd send me presents and flowers on a regular basis. He paid for everything whenever we went out, but it came at a cost. You were his. He had bought you and now he owned you. And so, the trips to the Big Market with Lola were most definitely off limits. The trips ended abruptly only a couple of weeks into my relationship with Tommy.

On my last girl's night out in town with Lola, I was walking towards a taxi and had to pass an innocent bystander, when Tommy came flying around the corner and attacked the poor bloke. He swore down that I was walking with the man and wouldn't listen to anything I had to say. The poor guy got a beating for nothing. The bystander was in a world of his own and Tommy started screaming, 'What are you doing with my lass?' He then punched the guy a couple of times in the face. The guy was in so much shock that he didn't retaliate, he didn't have time. He just kept saying 'What you on about man, I've done nowt wrong.'

I was shouting, 'I've never met the bloke in my life, leave him alone!'

Tommy's tunnel vision couldn't see the truth as he battered the guy stupid.

Tommy had apparently been following me and was convinced I was only down the town to pull. Any poor man who even got close to me was a threat to Tommy's pride and usually suffered some consequence because of it.

So, that was the end of my independence and nights out with Lola. It just wasn't worth the aggravation and questions. I most certainly couldn't risk another innocent man taken a hiding for walking anywhere near me.

Every weekend I now frequented the Westerhope Social with Tommy and his cousin Trev and wife Linda. Tommy was old-fashioned in the sense a woman was not allowed to go to the bar and never ever ordered drinks. He was insulted when I even suggested getting a round of drinks. I was working and earned decent money, I thought it was only right.

'Don't embarrass me Karen, women do not buy drinks,' he'd say. 'End of discussion.'

He even watched me like a hawk going to the toilet and suggested Linda go with me. What did he think I was going to get up to in there?

Like my dad, put a drink in him and you never knew what the outcome would be. But it was never pretty.

My parents had been my role models and I guess the scene was set, like attracts like; I was following suit and dating a man very similar to my dad.

At the end of the night, Tommy was a nightmare. He'd leave cigarettes burning in his hand while he fell unconscious on the settee, or sometimes wanted food cooked at 2am and wouldn't take no for an answer. He would shout at me even though my family was up in their beds sleeping. He was incredibly disrespectful considering this was our family home.

He started turning up unexpectedly in the middle of the night and would throw stones up at my bedroom window, drunk, making sure I wasn't with another man. He'd demand to be let in to see that there was no one else there. It was relentless.

It wasn't love; it was ownership.

The jealousy, controlling and overbearing behaviour was draining me, particularly because I was still living at home with my family. The whole atmosphere became tense and tiring. Getting accused of cheating for just looking in the wrong direction got me down. I honestly didn't have the stamina anymore and I became miserable and extremely depressed very quickly.

We had only been dating for about eight months and I spent the last few weeks wondering how to end this toxic relationship. I don't think Tommy was that happy either; he always seemed to be tense, always looking angry, never relaxed and happy. It was almost as if he preferred the chase and the resistance but as soon as I was *his*, and he had his trophy, there was no emotional effort required from him. Cold and callous, emotionally empty except for outbursts of rage to men that even dared look my way.

Yes, the gifts and the flowers still came, but at a price. It was a bargaining tool for his ego and to brag to his peers that I was his. That's when the novelty faded for me and although I think he would have stuck it out for longer, I was mentally exhausted and wanted out. I had three captors now and sensed I was deteriorating fast.

I finally plucked up the courage one morning as he was leaving my Mam's house for work. I said it was over. It was early December. I was expecting hell and damnation, but he took it rather calmly and looked me straight in the eye.

He said, 'Okay, so you're saying we are over.'

I said 'Yes, I'm sorry, I really am, but it isn't working.'

I was terrified he would come at me.

He didn't.

He calmly said, 'Okay then,' and walked out the door. Just like that.

All that worry for nothing, he had taken it really well. Or so I thought at the time.

I really had become low. The strain of years of drama and shattered dreams had taken their toll. I felt like I was swimming against the tide and never getting very far. I was weak and weary and drowning daily.

Christmas came and went, and my nineteenth birthday loomed. It was nothing like the year before with all the excitement and anticipation, the joyous attention bestowed upon me.

I had been talking about getting a bottle of perfume. All the girls at the salon were raging about it, Givenchy, and so I asked Mam if I could have it as my present. It was expensive, but she agreed and gave it to me on the morning of my birthday, though she reminded me that Dad hadn't helped with the cost.

That night I rang everyone I knew to ask them if they fancied a birthday night out with me. It was only three days after Christmas, and they all declined. I couldn't really blame them; after all, I had dropped my friends during the last eight months with Tommy. Not my choice of course, but just the way it had to be if I wanted an easy life without the agro from him. I called Linda, Tommy's cousin's wife, begging her to come out with me. Eventually she said yes. She knew a club where a band was playing, and we decided we would give it a try.

It was 28 December 1986. I had a bath and styled my shoulder length curly hair, all wild and tussled and put on a tube, a skin-tight black dress with stockings and stilettos. The past months had made me drop a lot of weight and I had started to like the feeling. I was at least in some kind of control over an uncontrollable life. I was restricting my food intake and I took lots of exercise. It was becoming a problem; I knew it wasn't healthy. I felt guilty if I ate a meal and took various medications to thwart my appetite to stay slim and in control.

I went to meet Linda and we had an all right night considering I was still rather low. I was relieved I wasn't with Tommy anymore and yet it still felt strange. I was adjusting again to my environment without someone doing all my thinking and talking for me. Logically it was the right thing to do; subconsciously I guess I was lost again.

I said my goodbyes to Linda and got into the taxi to come home.

Mam and Dad were still awake and looked to be in the middle of a fight, so I played my usual, 'I'll just go straight to bed,' routine and off I went up the stairs.

As soon as I walked into the room, I could smell the new perfume. I switched on the bedroom light and saw it lying in the corner of the dresser on its side with the top loose. There was a pool of it that had leaked onto the table and a large dark stain on the carpet on the bedroom floor.

Immediate panic took over. My mam had paid a fortune for this perfume, she would kill me if she knew it had been spilt.

'Amy, Amy what have you done to the perfume,' I said in panic mode.

Amy sat up in bed. She sniffed the air and looked over at the dresser and a look spread across her face. She was guilty. Whatever she had been doing with the perfume she realised she hadn´t replaced the top correctly. She had obviously knocked against the dresser in the darkness and the law of gravity had done the rest.

We were both thinking the same thing. Mam would go ballistic.

She screamed at the top of her voice, 'Maaaammmm, Karen's woke me up on purpose and I need to be up early tomorrow for my work placement!'

Panic and fear set in and I froze to the spot. I was trying to comprehend what was happening as I heard my mam charging up the stairs already effing and blinding, and she burst through our bedroom door. 'What the fuck have you done?'

Before I could utter a single word of reason, she laid into me. Punches flew straight to my head with both fists. She pulled at my hair with one hand and she gripped hard to steady herself while she punched my head with the other. She yanked my head down low and kneed me in the face, then let go and continued punching me with both fists. I lifted my arm up to cover my face as I always did, only this time, she hit my bony elbow and squealed out in pain. 'Brian she's just fucking hit me!' she screamed.

I heard Dad pounding the stairs like a mad man. 'She´s fucking done what?'

He ran into the room, that familiar look of rage on his face.

He joined in the melee. I tried to curl up in a ball as the two of them rained punches to my head and body.

It went on and on and on. I was still sitting where I had fell onto my sister´s bed. It seemed to last forever. The pounding noise in my head and the sounds that rang through my ears with every beating I ever endured was always the same. Thud, thud, thud. Lights flashing in my brain even though my eyes were tightly closed, feeling nothing but adrenaline and fear. But this was the worst yet. Four fists and four feet pummelling my head and my body, wounding every inch of me as a person, physically, mentally and emotionally. I can honestly say it was the worst beating I had ever had off my parents separately, and now collectively.

Sheer exhaustion on their behalf was the only thing that finally finished their attack. Then they started on me verbally. I heard the cunt word over and over again, useless, clumsy, ungrateful, worthless, selfish cunt. After a while I didn't hear them anymore. By then I had already died inside. What was left of my soul, battered since age four, now also disappeared. The flicker of hope in my heart extinguished.

They went back down the stairs. I gathered my tears and stopped, as I always did, and looked at my sister with contempt. I never said a word. I just unravelled my curled-up, fragile body and walked calmly into the bathroom with a lighter and locked the door. I literally slid down the wall behind the door and I knew. I knew it was never ever going to end. Whatever spark of hope that lived within me up until this point had gone. I just wanted out. Out of this war zone, out of this world and out of the endless pain that now had no limit to suffering.

I took a Bic razor and burnt the plastic off it with the lighter. I took the blade across my wrist and I sat back and watched the where my dress lay between my legs as it started to fill up with my blood. It wasn't black like I expected from such an evil person. It was bright red, just like other people's. That confused me.

I wrote 'sorry' on the bathroom door in my own blood for two reasons. Firstly, I was genuinely sorry for not being the person that they expected of me, whatever that was, I was sorry for never getting it right. I was sorry for being born so bad, sorry for clearly destroying everyone's life. I was sorry for my pitiful existence and I had meant it. *Sorry*.

The second reason was a personal one; I wanted them to keep that image with them imprinted in their heads forever. Calculating yes, but I honestly wanted them to feel some of the pain I had endured from them for nineteen years. I was incredibly calm. I sat back and was relieved that it would soon be over. I sighed, there was a strange euphoric inner calm. I was pleased with what I had done.

The movies made it look so quick and easy. You cut, you relax and then you're gone. Twenty minutes in and I was still waiting to die. I was thinking, should I not be seeing some kind of tunnel by now? Definitely deluded, I'd read way too many fantasy books and watched far too many flicks that portrayed the opposite to what I was experiencing.

'C'mon God, let me fucking die,' I whispered to myself. 'Get it over with, take me to wherever it is you are going to take me and make it fucking quick.'

He wasn't listening.

Yep. God had surely deserted me long ago as there was no tunnel or harp music, or anything. Just a sharp thud against the bathroom door where my family had now realised something was seriously wrong. I'd been in there for ages and they all started to panic. They're now trying to break down the door and the bloody noise, man. Nineteen years old and still can't get any fucking sleep.

10

Sickness and Sympathy
Flowers for Mam

I came to in the old RVI Hospital where they had a huge space cordoned off with curtains around dozens of single beds. No fancy single rooms in those days.

I heard the paramedic outside my curtain doing the handover to the doctor at A&E saying, 'This is Karen Slater, it's her nineteenth birthday today. Deliberate lacerations to her wrist, considerable amount of blood loss due to several cuts but tendons intact.'

He continued. 'She's been suffering from depression, untreated and not managed at this time, she has been celebrating, so consuming alcohol, but took no medications that we know of. She's otherwise healthy but quiet and withdrawn and, to be honest, we are a bit more concerned for her mother who is over there. She has had a terrible shock and is in a right state.'

What the fuck?

Seriously, I just couldn't believe what I was hearing. Oh my God. How did she manage that? She beat the shit out of me and then Dad joined in and between the two of them they've convinced the hospital that it's all the fault of their depressed, self-harming and selfish daughter. It's not like I could tell the truth. Who would believe me? I'm lying here in bed now with fear and confusion and disbelief. I'm also feeling guilty for how poor Mam is. How did she manage to make me feel like that? After all, it was her abuse and violence that started it all in the first place.

No point telling the doctors anything, they would have already come to their own conclusions. As they drew the curtain and cleaned and stitched me up, they were asking me questions.

'Yes, I'm depressed,' I said, 'I'm sorry, I don't know why I did it. Yes, yes, I know, sorry.'

Oh God, I feel even worse than I did before I'd done it.

I was sent home the next day and my aunt arrived from Dublin. My aunt always arrived if there was a need or a drama. Mam told everyone who would listen that she really needed her sister at that time which just made it even worse. Everyone was walking on eggshells and no one asked me anything. There were just the occasional whispers that stopped as soon as I walked into a room. My sister got sent home from her placement as she had been crying all day and flowers kept coming to the door for Mam, who needed the comfort and sympathy leave from work.

No fucking flowers for me though. Not that I expected flowers, but it was a strange feeling watching my mam receive them like a grieving parent whose sick daughter had just died. I wasn't dead and the person putting the flowers in the vases was my bloody abuser. I mean, really.

A few days in, the silence broke and my aunt said, 'How do you feel about coming to live with me Karen?'

Mam quickly joined in, It's a good idea.' She looked at me, 'Look, I'm worried when people do things like you've just done, they end up in the psychiatric ward in St Nicks and they never come out. The key is thrown away and we don't want that for you, do we? Besides, what would people think?'

I was at a loss for words as she continued.

'So, I think you should go and live with your Aunty Gina until it's all blown over.'

Her words sank in slowly. The thought of being locked up for the rest of my life, especially where my mam and dad worked, scared the hell out of me. I'd heard stories of people being locked up for less and never released again and they had become institutionalised, got to a stage where St Nicks was their home. Normality. Mam and Dad had talked about them sometimes. That was terrifying. My thoughts were racing as it started to sink in.

I started nodding my head. At least I'd be out of here, this fucking madhouse. I had been visiting Dublin on my own since I was ten years old anyway and I was more than familiar with the place. I'd loved it. I had spent hours playing in the farmer's fields as a child and stealing potatoes with my cousins. We laughed and we had fun, no one was waiting for the next assault.

Yeah okay, I thought, I'll go there. I nodded again and it was a done deal. Everyone looked happy, especially Mam who looked as if a huge weight had been lifted from around her neck. The filing cabinet in my head though, would process it properly later. My mind was starting to run away with me. *Am I that bad that I am being sent away? Would I really be stuck in hospital forever if I stayed here? Have I ruined my parents' lives that much that this was the only solution?*

No, there was too much interference in my poor head, and it was much better to file it away with the rest of the unthinkable and bury my head in the sand and look at the positives. Quick, train my brain, change my internal dialogue. I'm going on a long holiday to Dublin. That's all. Nothing more, just a long holiday.

Next day my aunt flew back home, and I would join her within the fortnight. I had to inform work and give notice and tie up the loose ends first.

Nothing was ever mentioned or talked about again. Nothing ever was in our home. I even convinced myself within days that I had reached this decision by myself and was now telling everyone that I had always wanted to travel and was leaving Newcastle to live in Eire. Within a week I was getting excited. Funny how my self-preservation hid the real facts… even from myself.

A day or two before I left for Dublin, Tommy had been on the phone asking if he could take me out. I didn't have the heart to tell him over the phone that I was going away, so I agreed to meet him that night. He turned up with red roses and he took me to a place in Newcastle which played Motown and Soul. I took off my coat as he brought over my drink and he asked why my arm was bandaged. All I could say was not to worry, it had nothing to do with him. I'm not sure what conclusion he came up with or if it made any sense to him because I had never once discussed my parents' abuse with anyone, especially him. I never even named it abuse until decades later. I certainly wasn't going to divulge that my injury was self-inflicted. He may have also thought I needed to be institutionalized, so I brushed it off and didn't give any explanations to him, nor did I have the heart to say I was leaving for good. I said I was going to Dublin for a month or two to clear my head and that I may see him when I was back. It was a strange and quiet night, but we left it on reasonable terms.

11

Dublin's Fair City - Therapy for the Soul

I boarded the plane to Dublin, and I ordered a vodka and coke. My friend. I sat back in my seat looking forward to my new adventure.

Dublin was like a breath of fresh air, we lived out in the countryside just outside of a town in Balbriggan. My aunt lived in an old country house up high in the Black Hills with only a handful of neighbours and where everyone knew each other well. There was no nebby council tenants screaming to keep the noise down. Just pleasantries and well wishes with the occasional crime update on who's children were now thieving Paddy's potatoes from the farm.

I had spent many a day out here in the country with my aunt and cousins as a child playing in the fields and now, here I was, an adult, noticing the real beauty of my surroundings for the first time. Beautiful horses grazing in the lush green, endless rolling hills with a backdrop to the sea, small animals darting between the trees. I could lose myself here and I did, just strolling down to the nearest road cleared my head and I could pretend all the bad stuff had never happened.

At first it was pointed out how nervous I seemed to be, how I'd jump out of my skin at every little sound. How I could never relax and flinched if someone moved too quick. They told me I was reserved and quiet, terrified to join in, in case I failed. It was pitiful, even in this beautiful free paradise I felt really trapped in time like that little four-year old girl, defeated and frozen inside my young adult body.

Over time I began to grow in confidence, slowly but surely and without the daily insults and harsh punishments. I was treated like an adult which helped me cultivate and evolve enough to join in conversations. I became aware that by holding eye contact with people, these became more meaningful, less superficial and helped foster a deeper level of understanding. I even felt several inches taller and walked differently, holding my head higher, not staring at the ground but taking in the beauty of my new surroundings.

I was obsessed about maintaining a certain weight though and had to do rigorous exercise every night or I would feel bad. I also still liked my friend vodka, but the rest of the family did too, so it wasn't too much of a problem. Though my consumption of the stuff was growing and starting to overtake even my Irish family's intake. The walls were adorned in rosary beads and everyone in Eire was into religion, so I rebuilt my friendship with my God. Much easier to have a relationship with a God when your life is going well.

I got a job in the local salon in Skerries and I would hitch to work, which was the norm for these parts in Eire. We'd go into town and socialise in the local pubs at the weekends and sing all the way home. It was like therapy for my soul, the laughter I had with my cousins and my new Irish friends was infectious. We drank, we sang, and we ate home cooking around a huge kitchen table with no fear of a dinner plate flying towards our heads. The log fire burned, and it was my home for two years.

It was the best time of my life.

The phone rang one Tuesday morning and Laura answered it.

'Karen, it's for you,' she called.' It's a man...he didn't give a name, just said he wanted you.'

I was confused. Who would be ringing me apart from my mam? I lived out in the middle of nowhere.

I answered the phone tentatively. A familiar loud and broad Geordie accent spoke my name. Oh no, shit.

'Eh, hallow Karen, is that ye? What you deein ower there, man?'

My body cringed as I heard the bellow of Tommy's overbearing voice. I held the receiver away from my ear to reduce the volume and answered casually, eager to get off the phone. We had nothing to say to each other as far as I was concerned. We never had. I listened for a minute and said, 'Thanks for calling, take good care. I have to go now.'

Receiver placed safely back onto the phone I secretly praised myself for leaving that man when I did. No reminiscing or regrets. Thank fuck, he couldn't come knocking on the door.

It was approaching May and my cousins were all loved up with partners. Our house was feeling small with sometimes ten adults all under one roof. One by one they each moved on to set up homes for their futures.

The boys were the first to leave the nest and then the girls; I was starting to wonder what I should do. Do I look for my own little flat or what?

A letter come in the post from Lola who was off to Spain to work and wanted me to join her. Perfect timing, I thought. It really was my time to fly the nest too and so I agreed over the phone to meet Lola as soon as I could.

Spain was an opportunity I couldn't miss; I sure as hell didn't want to go back home to Newcastle. Whenever I phoned, I was told that Mam was still getting sick every now and then and my brother was now getting the beatings that I used to get. My sister's survival made her Mam's best friend and confidant, mentored in the art of manipulation and control. I worried for them, especially my brother, he was only fifteen and lost. But I just couldn't go back, I had come too far. So, Spain was the next planned destination. I could get used to this travelling lark, I thought, as I started to pack my suitcase.

12

Sun Sea Sangria and Love

I arrived at Gerona airport about midnight on a Friday night and Lola, who I hadn't seen in two years met me at Arrivals. She was not her usual glamorous self, all dressed up and trendy, wearing the latest modern clothes. She was disguising what looked like a black eye under a baseball hat.

'Oh Jesus,' I said. 'What the hell has happened to you?'

'Car accident last week, it's nothing so don't worry about it, tell you later. This is Juan, he is our new boss, and he has kindly come to pick you up.'

'Hola Karen,' Juan said, smiling away and looking me up and down.

'Hi and thank you,' I said. Getting back to Lola, I asked, 'Car accident yeah, seriously, so what happened?'

'Well Juan was taking me sightseeing and as we were driving, we were looking out at the sea and at the boats and,' she nodded in Juan's direction, 'he went straight into the back of another car. Look.'

She removed the baseball cap and had some of her head shaved and it was stitched with staples. Not a little cut, a huge gash across the top of her head that could have killed her.

Christ, that immediately made me anxious; the same guy was driving us home. I was trying to look all chilled but couldn't take my eyes off her black eye and shaved hair and wondering if this Juan would be concentrating on the bloody traffic. He looked creepy and smarmy and seemed to be undressing me with his beady little eyes. And he was going to be our boss! Bloody hell. Not the best first impression I've ever had.

'Are you alright then?' I said.

'I am now you are here. Come on, we will drop the bags in and go out, the night club doesn't finish until 5am and all the workers go there after their shifts. I'll introduce you to everyone.'

We landed at an apartment that was heavily overcrowded which immediately shattered any illusions I had of our own beautiful villa with double rooms and an *en suite* and being in a beautiful destination, like you see in the brochures. Well, it was definitely nothing like that. No, as usual the reality was very different. Instead I stumbled into a shit hole fifty miles north of Barcelona and into what looked like a hostel. There were suitcases and clothes strewn all over the place. I immediately thought the place had been burgled. I had envisaged palm trees and white sandy beaches, turquoise water and us living the dream. I hoped it would look better in the morning. I dropped my case off and out we ventured into dozens upon dozens of pubs lining the narrow streets. Every cloud I thought.

The music was blaring, and the measures of vodka were huge I was beginning to warm to the place. Hungry and tired I was drunk soon after and the rest of the night was a blur. I have no idea who I got introduced to, and I had forgotten everyone's name by the next morning. Lola had very little money because she hadn't started working yet and I turned up with very little too as it had been such a hasty decision. We turned on our charm and ponced what we could before stumbling back home for some sleep.

I woke with a hangover and not much recollection, realising that the apartment was worse than I thought. Bodies asleep all over.

The first two weeks were spent living on Philadelphia sandwiches and pestering the life out of holidaymakers for vodka and coke, while waiting for our apartment change and our new job to start. The apartment change was most definitely a downgrade and had even more people living there than the last one which, funnily enough, now looked luxurious in comparison. We had two rails for our clothes and two single metal-framed beds with paper-thin mattresses and no window. It looked like a fucking prison cell. The fridge was that bad that I'm sure it was growing its own penicillin in there and was most definitely unusable. The stench when you opened it turned my stomach to the point of retching and I could never make out what all the green gooey stuff stuck to the inside was. Alexander Fleming would know.

There was no furniture, no pictures, no home comforts. Just beds and mattresses for people all paying 50 euro each week. I felt like Oliver Twist holed up with a Spanish fucking Fagin, but I suppose we at least had a roof over our head.

Our new job was in the darkest dive I had ever encountered and at one point I thought we would be trafficked for sex. Apparently, years earlier it had been jumping, with a great reputation for British tourists. The most popular pub in the town. Now it was owned by two Spanish brothers who probably worked in bookkeeping or auditing before acting on the desire to have their first pub. Big dreams and no experience, it was the blind leading the blind, hoping to make it a success. With dungeon-like features, dark lights and no windows, they were trying to appeal to hip young tourists, with a new influx of acid house music.

It was 1989 and everyone was tripping on ecstasy or acid or whatever they could get their hands on. Even the best drugs on the market couldn't make you enjoy this pub, though. Tourists were looking for fun which this pub definitely was not. I dare say, it may have worked in Glastonbury with the raves hitting the scenes. But this was Calella, for fuck's sake.

Still, we had a job and we could pay our rent. Our job was those bloody pests that you see when you're on holiday, trying to get people into the bar. You know, the ones you want to

scream *Fuck off and leave me alone* to.

We were two attractive Geordie girls with great banter and good at what we did, but the crowds we would bribe to frequent our pub were always put off by the darkness and dingy feel. With loud house music ringing in their ears they would sup their drinks and leave pronto. Occasionally I worked behind the bar, which I loved. We worked long hours and never had a day off and it was hard on the body. I'd wake in the morning, hung over, and go downstairs to the bar to have a Cider and Black to pull me around before I started my next shift. Most nights we would finish at around 2am and then all meet at the local nightclub called 'The Galleon', and that was our socialising and letting our hair down time.

My gums would bleed frequently, and I never had much of an appetite, yet my face looked bloated due to the daily drinking habit. I got less sun than if I had been home in England so was severely depleted of vitamin D. I had to drink alcohol to muster the energy for my next shift as we were permanently hung over and tired, but we got to meet some fabulous holidaymakers and partied every night without a break. It was not a healthy lifestyle, but it really was an amazing experience.

I had changed my job as the season slowed down and was now working in a British pub for a British boss who didn't feel the need to constantly linger and slime around my backside. It was a good family pub with a much healthier atmosphere. The weeks flew by and as it was approaching the back end of September the place quietened down and one night was to change my life forever.

A group of English lads from Brighton walked into the bar and my eyes locked immediately with one of them. I honestly fell for that man the very minute I saw him and practically ignored everyone else in the pub to just concentrate on him. His name was Bob and he was originally from London with a broad Cockney accent that I just drooled over. He had the bluest eyes I'd ever seen, and I couldn't stop staring into them. We spoke, we flirted, and he left, promising to come back the next day to visit me. I seriously couldn't wait to see him again. That night I staggered home with a smile plastered across my face.

His friends hated the resort and although they were booked for two weeks, they were now only planning on staying for one. I was devastated, but Bob came on his own to visit me every single day. Every night him and his friends came by, his friends probably out of courtesy and because they were bribed.

I was hooked, and the thought of him leaving was sad, but we promised to stay in touch and on their last day he said he would take me out for dinner. As he leaned forward to kiss me, I thought I was going to faint with nerves. I was sober and didn't know how to be around people in that condition, especially someone that made my stomach knot up and do somersaults. I stuttered when I spoke to him and just giggled like a school kid at whatever he said. We said our goodbyes and promised to stay in touch.

I couldn't stop thinking about him. I couldn't stop talking about him either.

Two weeks later I received a letter from him and was ecstatic to read he felt the same way about me as I did about him. This was the first man I had fallen in love with. I was twenty-two years old and my heart and body felt things I had never experienced before. Every single day I'd go to the pub under our prison cell of a home and ask if any more mail had come. The days it did I was as high as a kite and nothing could bring me down. On the days there was nothing, I stayed quiet but daydreamed.

The season was ending, the jobs were drying up and the bars now closing for winter. It was getting cold and we were all tired and pale skinned. Well, me and Lola were as we had just worked, partied or slept. We never did see the bloody sun! What little money we had left we needed to get home. By bus. We couldn't afford a flight. No money and no tan, but we'd had the experience of a lifetime and I'd met the man of my dreams.

And I needed to get home because I also had to revisit what I'd put off since leaving Dublin, when my smear had come back abnormal.

We eventually arrived back in Newcastle a couple of days later. There was nobody there to meet me. My parents were at the pub. No surprise there. I prayed they would be happy to see me since I'd been away for almost three years. Hopefully all the bad blood would now be a thing of the past.

We had spoken a few times over the years, but we never did know what to say to each other, so it was always general basic chit chat.

'How are you?'

'Fine. And you?'

'Fine.'

'How's the family?'

'Fine.'

'Ah, good, we're all fine then. Okay, take care. Bye.'

'Fine.'

I always had high expectations that things would be different. They never really were. But I always lived in hope.

I took a taxi back home. Mam and Dad came back from the pub and I shouted, 'Surprise!'

Luckily for me they were in a happy, merry mood and they genuinely seemed pleased to see me; besides, I had brought drink with me to ease the tension, (or escalate it depending on the mood). But everyone was in good spirits. We had all lived apart for some time now and knew this was just a steppingstone to be back at home and I did not want to overstay my welcome. Within days I was already invading their home and we were all beginning to feel the tension heightening.

My sister still lived at home, but my brother was now living at a friend's home. It was still in the same area, but a few streets away. It took some catching up to find out why.

He was now seventeen, I think, he had left school and was on YTS as a mechanic. He told me that after I had left the violence was put on to him and it became unbearable. He had to leave. He was withdrawn and still smoked cannabis, but he was getting by.

He still struggled articulating any kind of feelings and emotions, even general conversation he found difficult, being emotionally stunted and untrusting. My mam and sister were close, but the dysfunction was still there. Amy said she still occasionally had to duck from a flying plate of food and Mam's unpredictable outbursts still frightened the living daylights out of her. She had become Mam's carer, her best friend and her trophy. She did it all to save herself from a swift punch to the head. Her confidence was still on the floor and Dad still ridiculed her daily for her weight. She still had a nervous disposition, but she had given up the tablets and accepted the fact she would always be nervous and a worrier. She had swapped the pills for worry stones and beads that she kept under her pillow. Bless her.

Me and Bob were now in touch by phone and letter and I couldn't wait to see him. He clearly couldn't wait to see me either as he visited Newcastle for Lola's birthday party in November. He met the family and as we were getting ready to head to the party, he said I was beautiful. No one had ever said that to me before. Men had always said I was sexy, and they would love to give me one, but no one had ever said I was beautiful. I was touched. I wanted to cherish that moment forever. I didn't want to say goodbye.

No sooner had he left when I booked a bus ticket for the day before New Year's Eve to visit him. I started counting down the days. It was just as well as it was starting to get volatile in the house again. The more I hung around the more the dysfunction was sucking me back in. My three years of growing up and working on my self-confidence were diminishing before my very eyes and it was time to leave to keep my sanity intact.

New Year couldn't come quick enough. But the appointment at the gynaecologist hadn't produced good news. I had to have laser treatment on my cervix and quite intense treatment as my abnormal cells had been mutating whilst I had shrugged it all off and travelled to Spain.

I didn't want children at that point, so it hadn't concerned me that much, I was just relieved that Dublin had done a thorough examination while I was there and found it early.

I went in for the procedure as an outpatient with my nana as I wasn't allowed to come home on my own. After a few days of rest, I was back to normal and thinking ahead. Done and dusted and healing nicely I was ready to travel.

I boarded the National Express from Newcastle To London Victoria and daydreamed the whole way there about what it was going to be like seeing this man again and spending the New Year in Brighton, a place I had never been before. Would he still like me I wondered.

We met at Victoria station and I was mightily relieved as it suddenly dawned on me at the end of the journey that if he didn't turn up, I had no idea how I'd get back home. After the panic and relief, I was just smiling, delighted to be in his company again. There was no huge display of affection, my awkwardness never allowed it. But internally I was doing cartwheels to be with him. I was ecstatic.

It had taken best part of the day to travel to London and then London to Brighton but finally we arrived in the evening. Bob's accommodation was an attic in a large house, with God knows how many rooms, all rented out to mainly students. We were lucky, the attic had its own bathroom and a small area for cooking. With a bit of decoration and some moving of furniture it had the potential to be a lovely little first flat.

It was soon bedtime and I was terrified. I'd never slept with anyone while sober before. Especially not with someone that I wanted to be with. The whole concept was different. I had feelings and lust for this man but was awkward and unsure how to go about things. Fear had ruled my entire life and when I stripped back the bravado of alcohol, I was insecure and shy, terrified of rejection and abandonment, terrified of expressing any needs or wants. I climbed into bed fully clothed just in case. Good job he knew what to do because I didn't.

The days flew too fast and I didn't want to go home. He didn't want me to go either. It was 4 January 1990 and he left early for work. There was a bus back to Newcastle around lunchtime.

He stood at the door. 'Will I see you later or not?'

I couldn't promise him anything, as I really had to process it all. 'I don't really know Bob; I don't know what to do.'

All morning I wondered what to do.

I didn't really know this guy; we had only met a handful of times and it was a huge decision to make. I didn't have a job and only had a few pounds left after the festivities and I knew no one down here except Bob. As the day went on, I found myself rearranging every inch of his little attic and making it look like a little flat instead of a place for storing old furniture. I kept myself busy mulling over the whole thing which is my way of burying my head back in the sand. Should I, should I not? Can't think straight so keep cleaning Karen, I thought. But should I or should I not?

It seemed to take hours for him to return and at around 6pm I heard footsteps coming and climbing the stairs to the hatch in the attic floor. His smile when he peered his head through the door was one of pure delight and I guess I was here to stay. We fell into each other's arms, both nervous and excited at the prospect. This time I climbed into bed naked. I had made a little home and had a man loving me back. Tomorrow I would look for work and ring Mam to say I was staying.

13

New Beginnings

I was in love. I really felt I was in love. I finally ventured out on my own to visit my surroundings and to check out the narrow High Street just around the corner. The town was called Worthing, 30 minutes' drive from Brighton. Mostly retired folk and students lived there. I immediately spotted a trendy looking barber's shop. I remembered it had been in the local news for producing fashionable haircuts with character-themed shapes shaved into the back of boys' hair. The cuttings from the newspaper were stuck proudly on the windows. The salon even had its own water feature and looked amazing.

My internal dialogue was already starting to run its negative chatter, trying to talk me out of it by saying, *You're not good enough, you'll be exposed as inadequate, you'll be rejected, it's too fashionable for you, you´re still just a thick cunt.*

My self-doubt won. I would leave it for a day or two and I carried on walking, checking out the rest of the High Street before heading back to our little home in the attic.

My stomach was starting to flutter as Bob would be home soon and I was excited to see him. Every time I heard the footsteps climbing those stairs my insides had their own party. I told him about the barbers I had seen but how I was frightened to approach them, and I reminded him that I needed to find a phone to let my parents know that I was safe. We ate some dinner and then headed out to the phone box around the corner. I dialled the number for home.

Mam answered. 'I thought you were due back yesterday, did I get it wrong, is it today?'

'Hi Mam, no, I was due back last night but I've decided to stay down here and look for work.'

I immediately sensed she was sad which was strange as I thought she would be delighted. I was confused and now feeling guilty. 'Are you okay? 'I asked.

'No, not really,' she said.

This call was becoming awkward and I hadn't expected it to be. I tried to lighten the mood.

'It's great down here Mam, there's a fabulous barbers on the High Street and I've had a fabulous time Do you want to say hello to Bob?'

'No,' she answered.

'Okay Mam. Well look, I've got to go but I'll see you soon and ring when I can. Okay? Love you, bye.'

Everyone wants to make their family happy, but I tended to do the opposite. My mother had an incredible knack for making me feel guilty no matter what I'd done. Even when I hadn't done anything. I looked around at Bob with tears in my eyes. He put his arm around me and said everything will be all right.

Bob was trying to persuade me to go for the job in the glamorous barber's shop. 'You can do this, just go for the job. You can't lose anything by trying,' he said.

I was thinking I could lose my confidence and my pride. My fear of rejection resurfaced. But I decided to give it a go.

I was terrified walking to the barber's shop. Just before I turned the corner, I composed myself and put on my self-assured look. It's always served me well, like a duck on the water looking all calm and self-assured, serene even, yet paddling frantically under the surface.

I introduced myself, 'Hi, I'm Karen. I'm from Newcastle and was wondering if you have any positions available?'

I was wearing Bob's shirt as I only arrived with a few days' worth of clothes, but my hair and make-up were intact.

Antonio stepped forward, an Italian guy who took a mouthful from a can of Special Brew. I knew we'd get on once I saw the can.

We had a conversation of how much experience I'd had and where I had worked while he sipped from the can. Then he smiled and said I could have a trial after the weekend. I was delighted, it also gave me time to bus it home and collect some clothes.

I bounced out of the shop thinking, bloody hell, that wasn't too bad was it? Then my head said, 'Ah but will you be any good at it?' Sod off, I thought, I don't need to worry about that just yet. I went home to be the girlfriend and homemaker that I now was. I put my head through the hatch to the attic with a huge smile, and Bob said in his strong Cockney accent, 'Well done babe, told you, you would be alwight.'

The trial came and I was uncomfortable at first, but it soon felt right, and I was given the job. It became a great place to work. I needed some retraining on the barbering side and I could feel my face going red when I got something wrong, but I had nowhere to run so just had to keep facing my fears.

Every new thing I've ever done has been the same process. I take criticism very personal, even if it's helpful and yet I will work incredibly hard to become recognised and good at what I do. Within just a few months at the new shop Antonio called me into the back office and told me I'd done so well and was so well thought of that I was being promoted. I was asked to become manager and handed the keys to the shop. It was a massive achievement in such a short time, yet I never sang and danced or bragged about getting the position. My conditioning was that I should never show off as it wasn't nice. Nice girls didn't brag. So, I learnt to highlight my defects and play down my achievements to make other people feel better.

I loved my little job and little life and I had bought new things for the attic and made it homely. I bought curtains for our one little window and bedding, all matching, and I covered the two-seater sofa with the same material. I hung pictures of Marilyn Monroe and James Dean on our walls and partitioned the room, as apart from the separate bathroom everything else was in one room. When I was finished, we had a makeshift bedroom and kitchen and space for a little sitting room. It was all decorated black and white and trendy looking. I was really proud of myself and what I had accomplished.

Poor Lola had lost her drinking buddy again but we always kept in touch by phone and mail, and Tommy still occasionally turned up at my mother's pissed, saying he wasn't going to budge until she gave him details of wherever it was I lived. She was furious one morning when she found him asleep on her front step, drunk as a skunk and rang his dad to tell him that this behaviour was not going to happen again. Bloody hell, I thought to myself, relieved I lived so far away.

At the weekends we would visit the local pub or go out a bit further to see Bob's friends. He lived some distance from all his friends, who lived in Steyning about eight miles away. Apparently, this was because his mum chose the accommodation and put down the deposit and couple of months' rent in Worthing. This was to keep him out of trouble. I took it with a pinch of salt when he mentioned it in Spain but one night in our local pub, he enlightened me a little more.

He had been adopted from Northern Ireland as a six-week-old baby. His adoptive parents were very well do to and lived in Epping, Essex. He had no idea about his background and had only found out about the adoption as a teenager, which sent him off the rails and made him very conflicted with rejection and abandonment and, I guess, an identity problem. Also, the betrayal that he felt for having found out at a sensitive time, adolescence, had left him in inner turmoil that started his rebellion.

What's the best way to punish your high-status parents? Join a football hooligan gang and go to matches purely to fight. This actually horrified me as I couldn't work out why anyone would want to go and look for violence. The female part of me was outraged, seeing it from a women's point of view, thinking how frightening that must be for the everyday fan and family to have to watch that and wonder if they were about to be caught up in the middle.

During the fighting at one match, a rival gang member stabbed him, badly... to the point that they didn't think he would make it through the night. The hospital priest was called in to give Bob his last rites.

I sat there speechless. I was so in love with him that I had noticed the scars but hadn't seen them. Suddenly, I could see them clearly.

I said I didn't agree with any of the violence and didn't want to know any of the details. I was relieved he had left it all behind him but the thought of him being abandoned as a baby just made me feel terribly sad for him.

My own denial about my childhood made me think he'd had a hard start and I told him that. When he asked about my background, I said I grew up and wanted to travel so ended up living in Dublin and Spain. I really had compartmentalised my trauma for a long, long time. I told him nothing. When asked about the scars on my wrists it was because I was depressed and drunk and couldn't pinpoint the reason other than I had been impulsive whilst intoxicated. No need to elaborate, I thought.

It would be some time before I recognised my own shortcomings.

We cuddled tight that night. I was here to rescue him and love him better for sure, and I did. I adored this man, every day felt like a gift.

A few months in I noticed he would be looking for drugs on our nights out. The alcohol was enough for me but not for Bob. He liked to get high as well as drunk. His drug of choice at that time was acid and his favourite were called Purple Oms. I had read that they were dangerous but what concerned me more was he wouldn't take just one, no, he popped four at a time. We would go to raves and nightclubs and he'd be tripping, and I'd be drunk, and we just danced the nights away all weekend. While I nursed an occasional morning hangover, his comedowns and moods would last for days.

His parents wanted to meet me. They were going to drive up and stay in a hotel and take us out for dinner. I was a little nervous to say the least.

We arrived at the hotel and were led into the restaurant. I was surprised by their appearance. Bob was twenty-three years old, but his parents were considerably older than I imagined, possibly in their mid to late sixties. They looked rich and had an air of snobbery about them. Although they engaged in conversation with me, I could see they were not impressed. My hypervigilance as a child had taught me emotional intelligence and I read people's body language exceptionally well. A gift and a curse. There was no denying that they were just being polite in front of their son, but they did not approve. I couldn't understand why though, as I had never been in trouble with the law, and yet Bob had a charge sheet as long as his arm. I wasn't into violence and Bob was, I didn't take drugs and worked hard at my job. It's not like Bob worked in an office or was a solicitor, he was a roofer, so it didn't make sense to me. Yet it haunted me over the weeks and on meeting them for a second time. It confirmed that there must be either something wrong with me (and I still hadn't figured out what), or there was something else going on.

His father was arrogant and dismissed me at times and would roll his eyes if I spoke. He would correct my words and say I was wearing the wrong thing to dinner even though Bob was wearing an old t-shirt and jeans. He started nit-picking and then came the questions about Newcastle and the north south divide. Up to that point I hadn't even been aware there was north south divide. Christ, I lived in Dublin and visited Belfast in the eighties and hadn't come across this sort of interrogation. He kept going on about the lower class and to him, we northerners were most definitely lower class.

I was confused and insulted and didn't really want to join them for dinner again. The truth was that Bob's father had already formed his opinion about me before he had even met me. No matter how polite and courteous I tried to be, it was a waste of time.

'Bloody hell, that was hard work,' I said when we got home.

'What do you mean? What are you trying to say Karen?' Bob said.

'That was hard work Bob, your parents think I'm not good enough for you and don't like me. It was uncomfortable, and every time your dad took a pop at me you just sat back and let it happen.'

Already on the defence, he responded, 'Don't talk about my parents like that, do you hear me?'

His eyes widened with rage and his demeanour changed, his chest puffed out and he meant every word. I was taken aback as I hadn't seen this side of him before. It was daunting. I stayed quiet.

Our first disagreement, and a very touchy subject. It would become central in our demise. Thank God they lived far away, I thought.

It was early May when I visited my doctor. I wasn't feeling too well. I had sharp pains low in my stomach and was a bit concerned. I wondered if my gynaecology problems were returning.

The doctor was lovely and although she had no notes from my doctors back in Newcastle, I told her of my concerns and recent treatments, and about not feeling too well over the last couple of weeks.

'Could you be pregnant?' she asked.

I laughed nervously, 'I doubt it. I have just recently had intense laser treatment; I don't think I can get pregnant.'

'Nonetheless, we will do a test just in case.'

She handed me a sample jar and instructed me to go to the toilet and hand it back to her as soon as I had finished. I did as she instructed, and she told me to wait in the hallway. I was conscious of the time as I had to be back at work. This was wasting everybody's time. I looked at my watch. *I'm going to get hell from Antonio.* I took a seat.

I waited on the chair for what seemed like ages, getting more conscious of time and how my boss was going to react, when suddenly the doctor's door opened, and she popped her head around. She smiled. 'You're pregnant,' she said.

Holy fuck!

I didn't answer, I couldn't answer. I couldn't find any words.

'Come in,' she said.

'You are pregnant but I'm a little concerned with it being so soon after your treatment. The fact you have pain and discomfort in one side could mean an ectopic. So, we have to rule that out straight away as it is dangerous. I'm sending you up to the hospital in Shoreham to get a scan today.'

She smiled and wrote a letter out and asked if I was okay.

I quickly jolted back to life and said,' I don't even know where Shoreham is, and I'm meant to be at work, how will I tell them?'

She smiled again and explained how to get to the hospital and that reception would let me use the phone to ring work and inform them that I would not be in this morning. At times like this I was very aware that I never had parents I could ring for advice or support. Or comfort. Even with my recent laser procedure I had to confide in my nana, the thought of discussing that sort of thing with my parents was simply not an option.

I was very much alone in this department.

I was far away from home and now in Worthing Station looking for a train to take me to a place I'd never even heard of. I hated feeling weak and scared.

I was pregnant. I was in total shock. I had felt diseased and broken, how the fuck could I be pregnant? I was like a walking, talking zombie, asking people for directions as I tried to figure out which platform I needed to be on.

I held on tight to the brown envelope that the doctor had given me and when I finally found the hospital, handed it in and sat down in the waiting room. Time stood still. Everything was hazy. I couldn't get my head around it at all.

My name was called and off I went into a darkened room to have a scan.

'Okay Karen, so we are looking to rule out ectopic pregnancy, is that correct?' The radiologist said.

'Er, I guess,' I mumbled.

I climbed up onto the bed, lay my head on the small pillow and stared at the ceiling. My mind wandered back to a friend from Newcastle who had almost died when she had an ectopic pregnancy. She hadn't known she was pregnant and lost her fallopian tube in the process. Then I recalled Mam once telling me she had an ectopic pregnancy and how the baby had died.

She was really unlucky, she got everything, my mam.

The doctor's words jolted me away from my thoughts. 'You must be very early on because we can't really see anything, but I'm sure there is a very faint heartbeat right there.' She pointed to the black and white image which looked like fog on a broken TV screen.

'Just there,' she said. 'Very, very faint. We'd like to see you in two weeks' time to make sure, but any problems in the meantime come straight to the hospital.'

I nodded. Words wouldn't form. I was numb.

It was around 3pm and the whole experience had been going on from 9am that morning, yet it felt like only minutes. On my way home I was rehearsing what to tell Bob. I wondered if I should stay quiet for now. No need to worry anyone, that was my mantra.

My boss wouldn't be too happy, he'd only just made me manageress. I've only lived here four months and Bob, oh my God. I was in a cold sweat thinking about everything. No. I was going to keep quiet for now; at least until it was real, at least until it was confirmed for certain. It was a patch of fog today, nothing more, there's nothing certain just yet.

By the time I reached home I was exhausted.

I got home and had some food; I hadn't eaten all day. I was aware that someone was knocking at the door downstairs. It could have been for anyone, there was a dozen people in the building. I decided to go down to open it anyway.

It was Dee from work wanting to know why I had been in hospital all day and was I alright?

I blurted it out. 'I think I'm pregnant.'

Why did I say that? I hadn't planned to tell anyone.

'Oh my God, congratulations,' she said as she stepped forward and gave me a hug.

I protested, I told her not to say anything as it might be in the tube so it may not happen. It was probably best if we just kept it to ourselves, I said. She understood and was very kind. 'I won't say a word,' she said. We sat and had a cup of coffee.

Just as I was showing her to the door Bob arrived home. He looked at Dee and then at me. 'What's wrong?'

'Nothing, nothing,' I said.

'Just a girlie catch up.' Dee said her goodbyes and I closed the door behind her.

'Why was Dee here?' he continued.

'I wasn't very well at work and so finished a little earlier, she was just checking I was alright. I'm fine I will be back to work tomorrow.'

There was no point worrying him at this point.

Next day as I walked into work, Antonio asked if I was pregnant. Just like that. I was not expecting it.

'No,' I said, 'I don't think so. I just have some stomach problems.'

He looked me up and down, 'Mmm,' he said. And then in his very Italian accent, 'Dio mio, oh my God, I betsa you are pregnant.'

The next two weeks couldn't pass quick enough. I made my way back to the hospital for another scan and although I couldn't make out a thing on the tiny monitor the radiologist was clear that there was definitely a heartbeat and it was definitely in the right place, meaning I was definitely pregnant. It was not ectopic.

Oh my God, I was having a baby. I've made a baby with the man I adored, and the reality now was that it felt doable and really not so bad. Up until this point I had not even wanted to think it was possible, so I had dismissed it. But now I knew it was real and it was safe. I was going to have a baby and I was beginning to feel ecstatic.

I'd tell Bob tonight when he gets home. Everything was going to be just fine.

14

Out of the Frying Pan into the Fire

Bob walked in as he always did, around 6pm. I was sitting on our small wooden two-seater, staring at nothing in particular. I had been rehearsing what to say all day, but the words wouldn't come out. *What if he leaves me, what if he's angry?* I thought. *Surely, he has to be happy having a baby after what he's been through in life. Our own little family.*

But what if he leaves me…

'What? What are you looking so odd about?' he said. 'What's wrong?'

'Are you in a good mood or a bad mood?' I said

'Why?'

He half smiled which made me think he was in a good mood.

Here goes, I thought, *in for a penny in for a pound.* My mouth felt dry, I licked both lips and took a deep breath. 'Well… I've been to the hospital again today and…'

'Yeah,' he said, frozen to the spot.

'I'm pregnant.'

Time seemed to stand still. He looked dazed for a second or two, stunned even. Then he smiled.

Oh, thank God for that, I thought, as I jumped up to hug him. It was going to be okay; it was going to be magical and it was going to be perfect. We were going to have our own little family, full of love and happiness.

'I love you so much,' I said as I leapt into his arms, I couldn't stop kissing him.

'Are you sure about the baby?' he said. 'How do you know, why were you at the hospital, is that why you were there the other week?'

So many questions.

'Yes, I've known for a couple of weeks, but they thought the baby may be in the tube, so I didn't want to worry you. In fact, I didn't want to believe it at the time, so I kept quiet. I didn't think I could get pregnant after the laser treatment. But now it's real and you're happy and I'm realising what a blessing this could be for both of us.'

'Let's celebrate.' he said.

'What?'

'Just the two of us, me and you.'

We went to our local pub, just for an hour and we were both beaming. I'm sure the locals thought we were on something. We decided to not tell our families and definitely not Antonio…not just yet. We needed to get our own heads around the concept first. Bob just kept smiling to himself as he sipped on his pint.

I looked at him as he wiped a little froth from his top lip. I loved this man; I loved him so much I got butterflies every night before he walked through the door. I thought he was gorgeous; I adored his broad Cockney accent and we laughed together a lot. I'd stroke his arms, his hair, his neck...constantly, and I'd get a mild panic attack if he was more than ten minutes late. I would yearn for him to come home to me and then watch him pop his head through the hatch in our floor, covered in dirt from his job, and still be mesmerised. I thought he was gorgeous. I loved everything about him, even his scars, they were a part of him. I couldn't believe someone would want to hurt him or give him up as a baby. I wanted to cherish him and love him all better, for ever and a day. I had never loved anyone the way I loved Bob.

He let out a schoolboy grin as he wiped his mouth and placed his pint glass on the table. My heart fluttered. The thought of having his child and being able to give this baby what I never had and what his dad never had, made it even more special. Life was wonderful. I was so content; I had a great job and a good wage and a nice house and a man I loved. Roses really were growing in abundance around the door of our house with a white picket fence. Rented, with about ten other occupants, but still, that didn't matter.

A month went by and we acted out the role of a lovesick couple perfectly. We were constantly touching each other and holding each other tight, expressing our undying love for each other and for our baby.

Then the time came to tell our parents.

It was my turn first. I went to the phone box with Bob and rang home. I was a little apprehensive but excited and determined that no matter what anybody said, no one could hurt me or humiliate me. I was a young woman; a pregnant young woman who was soon going to be a mother and nothing or no one was going to stop that. I felt stronger than at any time in my life. I keyed in the numbers of the telephone. Mam answered. We shared a few pleasantries first.

'Mam,' I said, 'I have something to tell you.'

'What, what is it?'

'I'm pregnant.'

I could hear her take a gulp of breath.

She cleared her throat. 'Really? Really? Are you sure?'

My God, she sounded all excited.

'You sure?' she repeated.

'Yes Mam, of course I'm sure.'

Her voice...a little quieter as she turned away from the handset. 'George, George, it's Karen on the phone and she's pregnant.'

I heard him in the background, 'Oh God,' he said.

It wasn't how I imagined it would be. No objections, arguments or advice. For once we were all best friends and when I hung up, I was delighted. It couldn't have gone any better.

I turned to Bob and gave him a big sloppy kiss. 'Your turn,' I said.

He kissed me back. 'Not at the minute,' he said, 'I'll call them in a couple of days.'

I was bit taken back. This isn't what we had agreed. It spoke volumes; he wasn't comfortable with it. I left it as I was so relieved with my family's reaction that it was good enough for now.

Over the next few days, I couldn't help daydreaming a lot. I saw life differently. I noticed adverts on the telly with children in; they were smiling, laughing, playing with toys and eating chocolate bars. Suddenly the sort of ads that I'd never taken any notice of appealed to me. Baby equipment in the supermarket or pharmacy items kind of jumped out at me and smacked me in the face. I was so happy and so much wanted this baby. I was head over heels in love and couldn't wait. There was only one thing worrying me: Bob's parents and their reaction to the news.

It was over a week before he called them. After finally building up the courage to have the conversation with his parents he went to the phone box alone. He said it would be better that way, said he was nervous.

I waited in our attic.

Forty-five minutes later he returned. He tried to act all normal, but something was different about him and he couldn't even make eye contact with me. My heart sank. 'Well,' I said. 'What did they say?'

'Not much.'

'Not much? You've been gone forty-five minutes; you mean they're not happy.'

'They think we are too young that's all.' He shrugged his shoulders and sighed. 'They'll be alright, it's just a shock to them,' he trailed off.

He was cold and distant for the rest of the night. I felt rejected by him and his parents. Suddenly all my insecurities were back as I lay in our bed. He had turned his back to me. Normally we fell asleep facing each other, sometimes kissing gently, sometimes passionately. Not tonight. I lay awake for ages trying to figure out what it was about me that his parents didn't like. I had been polite to them; I had hidden my intolerance when his dad was not so nice. I had manners and despite the shit that life had thrown at me I was nice and always saw the good in people. I could never work out what it was about me that was so wrong.

I was always trying to change to fit in, trying to figure out what was missing so I could right it. Yet, people baffled me. I'd listen to someone like Bob's dad moan about things that I considered unimportant and think to myself, *Christ, there are starving people in the world and your soup is the wrong fucking temperature.* He'd bang on about how the northerners were so different. Once, he'd even called us scum and I had to bite my lip. I wanted to tell him that we all shit from the same place but of course I just smiled, nodded and mumbled something about it not being right to tar all northerners with the same brush because he'd met some less salubrious types in the past. He once asked me if my dad kept Whippets and had an allotment with pigeons. I couldn't be bothered to answer that question. He also said the air is full of pollution up north. All smog. Jesus Christ, I'd read somewhere that London was one of the most polluted places in the United Kingdom; just what planet was he on?

And yet none of that mattered now, there was only one thing on my mind. God only knows what he had said to Bob about this pregnancy with the Northern girl he hated so much.

I watched Bob carefully over the next few days, hung on his every word. As much as I hated to admit it…Bob had changed.

We were invited to Chris' house, a guy I worked with. He asked us for dinner with him and his wife and we had a great night. Bob drank a bit too much and was starting to get a bit cheeky so I asked if they could call a cab. We bid our farewells and climbed into the taxi. I'm not even sure what was said but rage was seeping from every pore in Bob's body. I then said something totally innocuous and he turned on me and slapped me hard across the face. The taxi immediately screeched to a halt, which threw us forward in our seats.

The taxi driver jumped out. 'I'm having none of that in my car. Do it again and I'll call the police.'

I naively hoped that the cabbie's outburst may have snapped Bob back to reality. No chance.

'Call the fucking police,' he snarled at the driver. 'They don't bother me mate, no fucker bothers me. Not you, not the police, no cunt.'

I was scared there was going to be a confrontation but probably more embarrassed than anything else. I said we would walk the rest of the way and paid the driver. I had never seen someone change so dramatically and so quickly. I tell a lie, of course. I'd seen people change like that, after all I grew up with parents that changed like the wind but that was standard behaviour. With Bob, I had only seen loveliness and affection and now suddenly he had changed. I had never witnessed these outbursts before. As we started to walk home, he was cold. 'Why did you do that? Now we've got to fucking walk home.'

'Because you were embarrassing and you would have got arrested, that's why. That taxi driver wasn't having that happen in his car.'

Bob walked a little way ahead and then turned around. 'My old man says you've done this on purpose. You've tied me to a ball and chain to keep me and you're going to ruin my life.'

I couldn't believe what he'd just said. I was livid. 'Ruin your life, ruin your life? How can I ruin your life? It's you who has the criminal background Bob, not me! And what is there to fucking ruin? It's not like you were living it up in the Ritz before you met me.'

His face contorted with rage. 'You've trapped me, you fucking slag.'

He took a step towards me. I stood my ground and refused to budge. As we came almost nose to nose, he punched me in the side of the head, and I fell to the ground.

I was enraged, I'd never been so incensed in my life. I jumped up quickly and ran over to him as he walked away. Without even thinking, I punched him as hard as I could in the back of the head. He staggered a little, clearly shocked. Then he came at me and again punched me in the side of my head. Again, I fell. I was dazed and didn't hit him again. I knew this was one fight I would never win. I was stunned. There was no real pain, just shock. I was on the ground, back in familiar fucking territory, it was happening all over again. I was back in my parents' house, on the bedroom floor.

That familiar feeling was back with a vengeance, like it had never gone away. Even the pounding in my head was the same as I remembered.

'Oh fuck,' I muttered to myself. 'It's happening all over again.'

His words brought me back to the present. 'And you're not getting in the fucking house either, you can sit on the step and fucking freeze to death for all I care.'

I was still on the ground trying to process what had happened. How was it possible that I was back in a place I thought I had left for good? How did I not know it was coming? Or did I know but refused to really know? Had I missed the obvious signs?

Tears streamed down my face as I raised myself to my knees and sobbed like a child.

I was scared, I was cold, I was pregnant and in a strange place and he had left me all alone. The man who I adored, the man I was ready to build a life with. He was tearing my dreams and my hopes apart. Fuck his dad. This was his doing.

I waited around in the cold for at least twenty minutes until he had gone, then made my way home, hoping he had left the door unlocked. I had no idea what to do or where to go if he had locked me out.

Luckily, the main door was on the latch. I crept as quietly as possible into the house and up the stairs to our attic. He had passed out on the bed, snoring like a bear. I climbed into the other bed and cried my heart out. My longing to belong within a normal, happy family was shattered once again.

I woke up during the night. There was something warm lying next to me in the dark. He had climbed into the bed I was in. I was so hurt and yet I clung to a slither of hope, relieved he was next to me with his arms around me.

I could think of nothing but my upbringing, my shit fucking childhood and the cold, brutal teenage years and I was right back there in the moment.

I always knew what my parents were doing was wrong, but I didn't know how to make it stop. I was taught to respect your elders and parents, no matter what. I had felt trapped and helpless and didn't know where to turn, longing to be grown up so that I could escape.

This, this scenario was so different, this wasn't meant to be happening. He was my boyfriend, my lover, the father of a little baby growing inside me and he had hurt me. He had torn out my heart in one night and reawakened my buried memories of beatings and ridicule. I felt hollow; my heart had been ripped out of my ribcage. I was haunted by pain and memories as I lay in the quiet night. I couldn't sleep, the turmoil was too much. I had to stop this pain that I was feeling. I had no doubt that it was wrong and this time I had choices.

And yet I chose to stay and not face up to the fact that my partner had battered his pregnant girlfriend and abandoned her in the middle of a strange place.

It wasn't too hard. I simply slotted the incident, along with the others, into that big fat, overflowing filing cabinet I kept locked in my head. Labelled, 'Pending.'

The sun was beginning to rise and as it always did, it made the hauntings fade.

Bob came to from his drink-induced sleep all remorseful and apologetic. He kept kissing me and promising me it would never happen again. He couldn't understand why he had reacted that way. He put it down to fear and drink. I suppose he reassured me. It was what I wanted to hear but I felt vulnerable and weak. Vulnerable because of the position I was now in and weak because I chose to turn a blind eye.

On his way out to work he gave me £40 and told me to go out and treat myself. He told me he loved me more than anything in the world and left.

The morning felt eerie, it felt like grief. I was grieving for the hopes I had dreamt only twenty-four hours before.

I got dressed and went shopping but I couldn't think straight. I hated this feeling, I felt transparent and like the world could see right into me. They could see the brokenness and bad that lurked under my skin. It was taking longer than usual to shift this state of being. Try harder Karen, I thought to myself. Think baby Karen, let's look in the baby shops and think happy thoughts.

I walked into Mothercare and looked at the tiny clothes for an innocent little baby. The babygro's seemed too small. I put one over my shoulder and looked in the mirror, trying to visualise myself with this tiny little being. All the love that I had to give would be directed to this child. It will not be punished, I said to myself. Nobody will hurt it, no one will ever lift a finger against my child. It will be loved and protected, not shamed and blamed, beaten or humiliated. My baby would know it was special and nothing else mattered. I was far too early into my pregnancy to buy anything but spending the time in Mothercare had taken the edge off my pain and my sore head, which was by now throbbing. I bought myself a pair of shoes and a t-shirt for the price of my shattered hopes and dreams.

It was a relief to be back at work the next day. Some normality resumed, and the salon was busy as well. At this point I had still not told Antonio that I was pregnant, but I knew he knew by the way he kept looking at me. I had no due dates or anything and I was still having light periods, so until the baby could be seen and measured properly by the radiologist there was no reason to tell people.

Bob kept having little outbursts of intolerance and anger at stupid things. They were becoming more regular with shorter time-periods between outbursts. One day we were in the car going out for the day and the traffic was moving slow. He started swearing and waving his hands about. I could see his rage simmering, like a kettle on the boil. Everything and everyone seemed to piss him off. I was on tenterhooks and told him to stop swearing at the other drivers. I was tense and on high alert.

'You don't fucking like it, get out,' he screamed.

I took a deep breath, tried to be reasonable. 'I don't know where I am Bob.'

He looked at me and snarled through gritted teeth, 'I don't give a fuck, I really don't give a fuck.'

I bit my lip. I think my silence infuriated him even more as he screeched to a halt by the side of the road. 'Get out now, get the fuck out!'

'No Bob, I don't know where we are.'

'Get out, get out now.'

I refused, terrified of his reaction but also terrified of being abandoned on a busy road with no idea how to get home.

All I could say was 'no'. I kept repeating, 'I'm not getting out; I don't know where I am.'

In the end he gave up, started the car and drove off.

Everything about Bob had changed. Only weeks ago, I'd get all excited at 5.50pm, waiting for him to come home. I didn't look forward to 6pm now, I was wary. Those butterflies had disappeared and were replaced by worry cramps.

The novelty had worn off for Bob too. He would only come home at seven or eight, sometimes even eleven or midnight. Sometimes he wouldn't come home at all. He was Mister Unpredictable, and it was extremely unsettling.

My nervous tension was back, as was my loss of appetite. When he didn't come home, I couldn't eat a scrap.

The new incidents of 'Bob rage,' was coming at regular intervals.

We had been invited along for a night out with Bob's friend, Tim. Tim wanted us to meet his new girlfriend, Terri. Bob announced at the dinner table with a big grin that we were having a baby. He seemed happy about it again and got us all to raise our glasses to toast the baby's health and happiness. Obviously, it was the drink talking. Me and Terri got on like a house on fire and chatted all night. Bob proceeded to get more drunk and started working himself in the taxi queue in front of Tim and Terri.

He was pointing at people in the queue calling the lads cunts and faggots.

'And he's a cunt,' he said, pointing to a man climbing into the taxi.

I was petrified that someone would turn on us; it was surely only a matter of time.

I grabbed him by the arm and tried to reason with him, 'Bob, for Christ's sake, you're going to get us all beat up.'

He looked into my eyes. The venom and hatred had returned. He turned to Tim and Terri. 'This is my ball and chain, she is ruining my fucking life.'

'Bob, stop it,' Terri chipped in. 'You don't mean that.'

'Oh, I mean it,' he said. 'Fucking trapped me she has, going to make my life miserable.'

Tim bundled him into a taxi and within a few minutes he was fast asleep in the back seat.

Terri was lovely; reassuring me that it was just the drink talking and everything would be all good the following morning.

The next day when I woke, I decided that I would save as much money as I could and work all the overtime offered. I wasn't sure what was going to happen to me and Bob, but I had to at least start getting a Plan B in place. The only person I could talk to was Dee from work. Though she said she was sad if I did have to leave, she also knew there would be a manageress position and she was the perfect candidate. I didn't blame her.

I was due some holidays from the shop and I booked them for September. I thought it would give me more time to save and with each month I worked, I got another day's holiday which bought me more time.

Life in our little house resumed to some semblance of normality unless Bob rang his parents, which inevitably put him in a bad mood. Luckily, he didn't ring home that frequently.

I still loved this man and was hoping that he would see that things could be really good if he wanted them to be. He hadn't assaulted me since the taxi incident, but it had changed my view of our future together. We were no longer a lovesick couple planning for our little family.

It was the summer of 1990 and England were playing in the Italia 90 World Cup and were doing exceptionally well. The eighties had been a dark time for football and hooliganism had been rife, but as England players progressed through this tournament the nation was gripped. Each time England won another match, they got closer to the final and people were celebrating in the streets with parties and held flags and banners of red and white. The colours adorned nearly every house in England and the country was excited about the possibility of England bringing the cup home. TV pictures showed celebrations across the nation. On the day of the semi-final, people were jumping in the fountain on London's Trafalgar Square to cool down as it was red hot. Crowds were dancing in the streets, the men shirtless and chanting songs. The smell of food on barbeques cooking filled the air, and everyone was merry and happy. Stillness fell on the country as England started to play the most important game yet, against Germany, in the semi-final. The tension was high; even I was watching the game on the edge of my seat.

Gazza got the ball in the centre circle and a German defender tried to take it from him. He overran and stretched out with all his might as Thomas Berthold came across… and went down. Gazza was booked. All our hearts skipped a beat with every wobble of Gazza's bottom lip. The commentator announced that if England got through to the final Gazza would miss it, and at almost the same time Gazza realised it too. The tears started to run down his cheeks and the country felt his pain and cried with him. There was something so honest and noble about Paul Gascoigne that day, it was almost good to see a man so sensitive, so proud and caring. I was proud to be a Geordie right there, right then.

But Bob was nowhere to be seen. I had watched the match on my own, he had left for work in the morning and still wasn't home by early evening. I made my way to bed but couldn't settle.

He eventually strolled in, early the next morning. He said he had been to London's Trafalgar Square to celebrate the match.

'Must have been nice,' I said somewhat sarcastically.

'The atmosphere was electric. Charlotte was there too,' he said casually.

Charlotte was Bob's ex-girlfriend. I couldn't say anything, what was the point and why had he even mentioned her?

He had made my mind up for me. He had mentioned Charlotte for no other reason than to hurt me, to cast seeds of doubt into my head.

I knew what I had to do.

As soon as I could, I rang Mam and asked if she'd mind putting me up for a little bit until I could get some accommodation. I don't know if it's because I was having a baby, but Mam was nice and said I could stay as long as I wanted. I could have our Stephen's old room.

'Is everything okay?' she asked.

'Yes, fine.'

'Fine, that's fine then,' she said.

I was leaving our little home in Worthing and I would be heading back home to Newcastle. I called at the National Express station and bought a one-way ticket for the following week.

I never told Bob I had my ticket, I never told work either. I told Antonio that I was taking my holiday in Newcastle. I thought long and hard and figured I'd tell Bob a day or two before I left. I felt sad but there was no turning back. I had made the right decision I just had to carry on as normal for a few more days.

It was a Sunday morning and I asked Bob if he wanted to go for a walk down the seafront for a talk. I loved it down there, listening to the waves crash into the pebbles whilst deep in thought.

I was nervous but very calm and as soon as we sat down on the front, I took a deep breath. 'I know you're finding this difficult and I never intended to make you feel trapped. I love you so much but the thought of you thinking I did this to trap you has really concerned me.'

He looked me in the eyes but remained silent.

'I've booked a ticket; a one-way ticket and I'm going back home. I don't want you to feel under any pressure. I am keeping this baby and believe me I'm quite happy and more than capable to do it alone in Newcastle, surrounded by family and friends.'

He stayed still, motionless, almost shocked.

'We can keep in touch and if you decide you do want to be part of our lives then you'll know where to find us.'

His eyes filled up with tears though he didn't shed any.

'When are you leaving?' he finally said.

'The day after tomorrow.'

I could see that he was taken aback, he hadn't been expecting it. He was shocked but kept quiet.

Two days later I boarded the National Express once again, and this time I headed for home, to uncertainty, yes, but with a belief that I would get through this next part of my journey for the sake of my unborn child.

15

Hope is a Good Thing

The National Express pulled into Newcastle and I was met by Mam, Dad and our Amy. My God, I wasn't expecting such a welcome committee. I was relieved to be back in familiar surroundings and delighted with the family welcome. They were all excited to see me and showered me with kindness and genuine concern for the baby.

I wasted no time in looking for accommodation and checked into the local doctor's and hospital to get everything back on track. I finally got a due date. My baby was to be born on New Year's Eve.

Fucking typical, really. I had been surrounded by drinkers and parties and madness my entire life and my baby was going to be born on the maddest day of them all.

Me and Bob kept in touch, but I got on with my life as time would not be waiting. I eventually got the courage to call Antonio and thanked him for everything he had done for me but also, that I would not be back as I was pregnant and having pregnancy problems.

'I knew it, I knew it,' he said.

He was angry and disappointed and rightfully so, but I had bigger things to worry about.

All I could do was apologise. I hadn't meant it to happen like this, it wasn't planned.

This was the closest I had ever felt to my family and I settled in well. It was comforting. Dad still looked for his trolley in the middle of the night, pissed in my bed occasionally and Mam could still stop you in your tracks with a cutting comment, but I handled it. It was the most stable I had ever known. Bob would ring and say how much he missed me and how different life was for him now that I was gone, but he mostly rang when he was drunk.

I finally got a flat in Gosforth and started to decorate it with my parents' help. It was in a high-rise block, but I was just pleased to be back in Newcastle. Mam and Dad even bought me a second-hand washing machine and we hung curtains. I was thrilled to bits. I was actually building a relationship with my parents.

By the time we were almost finished decorating, Bob announced that he couldn't live without me and said he would be joining me in Newcastle the following week. The thought of me moving on without him clearly shattered the illusion of that ball and chain around his neck. The phone calls that we had over the weeks were mostly about me being excited about the flat and how things were progressing nicely. He would ring drunk and say he missed me, I would tell him I'd been painting all day. 'It's starting to look lovely, oh and the baby has started kicking.'

A little food for thought.

He turned up at Mam's a week later with a car full of belongings and said he would help me finish decorating. I was excited to see him but also secretly apprehensive. This man that I fell in love with had already hurt me and let me down a lot in a short space of time. But all I could judge it on was my parents' marriage and how every relationship must be hurtful at times. I was a little nervous right up until I saw him smile, that smile that just made me want to kiss him and be close. I would look at his face and melt. I'd long for his touch like it was in the beginning, all loving and tender but passionate. When we hugged so tight, I couldn't breathe, like two teenagers, smitten and uncontrollable with our sexual urges.

He got out the car and said, 'Awight babe?'

He was back, I loved it when he said that.

I couldn't wait to show him all the work me and Mam had done on the flat. It only needed a touch more paint on the woodwork and finally it would be complete. If I say so myself, it looked fabulous. We pulled on our overalls and made a joint start. After a couple of hours painting Bob went to put the lid on the paint tin and couldn't manage it. 'Fuck, fuck! he screeched.

It was sticky and dented, clogged up with old hard paint. I looked over and laughed.

Out of nowhere he hurled the entire paint tin across the room.

My stomach knotted immediately. I was devastated. I had dared to dream that by some miracle my absence may have made him realise just what he was losing and that he might have changed and reigned in that temper of his. No. It was there and clear to see. I was crushed. I looked around the flat.

Me and my family had been decorating it for weeks. We had turned it from a shithole into a palace. Now there was paint everywhere. I couldn't believe it, the first day Bob arrived he had lost it within a few hours. He clearly had no respect for the time and money that had been put into it. But it was more than that. He had no respect for me. I had told him exactly the effort I had put into this place, why had he done that? It was a warning sign that I ignored. He had lost it again and this time it hadn't been because of a sensitive phone call with his mum or his dad, it was over a stupid old paint pot.

I should have given him his marching orders there and then. But I didn't.

I told him not to worry about it. 'I'll clean it up,' I said. 'It's just a little paint.'

I clung to the fact that he would be different after the baby was born, naïve yes, but hope is all I ever had to go forward with in life. I remember a Morgan Freeman line from the *Shawshank Redemption*: "Remember, hope is a good thing, maybe the best of things, and no good thing ever dies."

That was me, always hoping for things to be better. When they weren't, I went back in denial.

Bob got a job in a kitchen fitter's shop and we moved into our two-bedroom flat. It wasn't long before he was drinking and smoking the occasional joint again, and things always got worse after he had rung home.

He would go for days and days not talking to me and it was tense, to say the least. I never mentioned it to anyone, how could I? It would spoil the illusion. I just worked harder at trying to please him and adapting to keep the peace.

I was eight months pregnant when he attacked me in our bedroom. There was no reason for it. He just yanked me out of bed and grabbed me by the throat and pinned me up against the wall. I was on the verge of passing out as he tightened his grip around my neck. I was terrified he would hurt our baby. He punched me a couple of times to the side of the head then as quickly as it started, it stopped. Just like that. He said he was going out for a walk to cool down. I quickly rang home and Dad met me at the doorway to the flats. As soon as I walked into Mam's and explained that Bob had lost his temper and strangled me, she rang Denise and asked if she could help.

In hindsight I think my parents were afraid and didn't know how to comfort me or how to fix the problem. They had spent their own lives battling and sweeping everything under the carpet to make the bad things simply disappear.

It was the middle of the night. My friend Denise drove over and picked me up to take me back to her place. I stayed awake for hours with random thoughts that didn't make sense. I wondered what I should make for tea the next day, where would I put the cot, where will I get a childminder from when I go back to work.

Occasionally I would try and piece together what had actually happened, why he had attacked me, then I would go back to my random thoughts, will the cot fit in that alcove at that angle?

My coping mechanisms for blocking out pain was a normal reaction now. Prompt and effective but with lasting consequences.

The next day Denise took me home and asked Bob if she could have a word with him. Apparently, she said that if he ever hurt me again, he would be made to pay for it, and she meant every word.

Things settled for a little, but it was like living in a minefield. Put your foot in the wrong place and there would be an explosion.

Our baby was late, thank God, so New Year came and went, and I was to be induced on 14 January 1991.

We welcomed our daughter, Devon Eliza, into the world. She weighed 6lb and 13oz, not as small as the doctors had thought she would be, considering I was so tiny. She was perfect. Absolutely perfect.

I couldn't believe that this little human had been made by me and Bob. I loved her instantly and wanted to protect her forever. I never once took my eyes off her.

I wasn't as confident on the ward as the other mums were. They seemed to naturally know what to do. I didn't and I'd doubt myself a lot, constantly asking a nurse or the midwife for direction.

All the family and friends visited and even Bob's mum and dad drove up from London to see their grandchild. It was awkward and obvious that me and his dad didn't see eye to eye, but it was agreeable, and he was polite most of the time.

I stayed in hospital for a week before I left and brought our daughter home. It was a beautiful feeling and I was almost certain that the bad past was behind us. We tried to settle into some kind of routine, but it was a lot more difficult than I had anticipated. Bob had to go back to work, and that's when I noticed it.

Me and Devon were at our best, calm and adjusting and figuring it all out when Bob wasn't there but as soon as he came in the house it was as if she sensed that there was tension in the air. Something changed. She would become irritable and unsettled; this would make me nervous and I'd frantically try harder to soothe her as to not upset her daddy who had been at work all day.

This became our norm for a little while. Bob would make it very clear that the crying when he returned from work was not ideal. One day he walked through the door, removed his shoes and Devon started crying her eyes out. Without a word he put his shoes back on and went straight back out, slamming the door behind him. God only knows where he would go as he didn't know the area, but he would be gone for an hour or two.

The sleepless nights had us both worn out. But this is part and parcel of the process I thought.

By now I was doubting myself even more as a mother and the pressure to console a baby to make Bob happy was more than challenging.

16

Terror

One night that will haunt me forever was when Devon was teething. She just wouldn't settle. I was shattered and sitting on the bedroom floor with her in the single room, trying not to wake Bob in the other room.

Suddenly he appeared in the doorway. I looked up and mouthed, 'I'm sorry.'

He looked at her and then to me and calmly said, 'If you put a pillow over her, no one would ever know.'

My blood ran cold, the hairs on my neck stood up and the tightness in my chest made it hard to breathe. I started to hyperventilate.

I had no words. I didn't want to believe what I had just heard. Had I even heard right? Can a father really think like that? Did I misunderstand? Why would he say that? It was too chilling to even think about.

I couldn't leave him with her. I never had, and I never would. Call it a mother's intuition but it was never going to happen. I was exhausted and terrified that something was going to happen to my baby, yet my blueprint for life made me minimise the bad and hope for best. A survival mechanism of not comprehending the immediate danger we were in.

I just kept setting the bar higher for myself and became a people pleaser at any cost, to keep us safe.

I would try not to sound all gooey to the baby when Bob was around. Those moments were in private and when I did fall asleep it was restless, light and full of nightmares.

The energy in the house was rigid and it was inevitable that the day would come when I would accidently step on one of those landmines that littered the place.

That day came on 17 July 1991. Our beautiful baby was six and a half months old, on the verge of sitting up by herself. It had been a normal day and I got a pack of frozen chicken breasts and chicken legs out of the freezer to defrost for the following day.

Bob came home early from work, but he had been moody for days. He said he missed the south and his friends. He had brought in a bottle of vodka and some cans. Bad sign. Red warning flag.

I bathed the baby and put her down for the evening. It was an uncomfortable night and was about to get worse as he was downing the alcohol as if there was no tomorrow; the man was clearly on a mission. He was irritable and full of self-pity.

It was about 8.30pm. He rang his dad. I poured myself a large measure of vodka, I sensed something was going to kick off. I never even looked at alcohol normally, as I was still up through the night feeding Devon.

By time he came off the phone he was in an even worse mood,

and so it began. 'You've taken me away from my family, I never asked for this.'

I calmly replied I hadn't made him do anything.

'Yes, you did, by getting fucking pregnant, that's how. My life is fucking ruined.'

I took a mouthful of vodka. 'Why do you start every time you come off the phone to your dad? Why Bob? I never begged you to come here and I've never begged you to stay. What the fuck is it your dad says to you to cause this kind of reaction?'

'He says you've fucking trapped me and brought me up to a shit hole, that's what.'

I smiled, 'Well he would, wouldn't he? He's a fucking snob.'

Big mistake on my part saying that, huge mistake, in fact. Boom! The landmine was well and truly detonated.

He threw his glass across the living room towards me. I managed to move my head quickly to the left and it smashed off the wall above my head. He jumped up to his feet and grabbed me by the hair, dragging me off the settee. I was on my knees squealing for mercy, but he pulled me up to my feet and punched me straight in the face. I had taken some beatings over my twenty-three years of life, but I had never been punched in the face with such force. Bob, in his head, was back on the terraces fighting twenty- and thirty-year-old men. My parents' punches and kicks paled into insignificance. I felt disorientated, but quickly steadied myself, trying to look less vulnerable.

He appeared to take stock for a second. I thought it was over but then his face changed, and he launched into a sustained, frenzied attack, calling me all the cunts and slags under the sun.

This beating was to be different. It would continue long into the night.

He looked possessed. His pupils were dilated and jet black, the blue eyes I once loved had gone. He had a vacant look about him, trance-like, a mad man. He was screaming insults and walking away, then running at me to punch me or drag me to the floor. He would walk off again and pace the room, only to return with force. I'd be crying, all curled up, thinking it was all over. Occasionally he would go silent, his breathing laboured, then a rush of rage and adrenalin made him come back to attack me again.

'I'm sorry,' I'd beg, 'I will never say that again.'

It didn't matter. He didn't hear me; this was not Bob; this man took on a whole new identity of his own. This was a man who hated at the football matches, the one that hated his real mother for abandoning him, the one that hated the bastard that had stabbed him and left him for dead. This was a real-life dangerous man that could kill me in a blackout and not remember a thing. Gone was the Bob I loved. His wounds from the past were now in control and I was paying the price. This was pure hate and he was taking out his entire life's hurt and anger on the mother of his daughter.

He disappeared into our bedroom and I saw an opportunity to ring the police. I quickly ran to the phone, but he was back. He punched me so hard I dropped the phone. He then pulled out a survival knife and cut the phone line in half. Oh, dear God, he was going to kill me.

The knife was like the one Sylvester Stallone uses in the movie Rambo. One side is serrated and saw-like and on the inside of the handle is a compass with a wired line for fishing. A real, genuine hunter's knife. He'd shown me this once before, down in Worthing, but now he was hunting for real and I was the prey.

He dragged me by the hair all the way down our passage to the front door and made me sit on the floor. He held my face and pushed my head into the wood.

'Now Karen,' he said, 'we are going to play a game. It's called *Moving Target.*'

I nodded, unsure of what else to do.

'I close my fucking eyes and if you move, I stab you to death. So, don't fucking move. Is that clear?'

I nodded my head as the tears ran down my face.

He closed his eyes and lunged towards me as the knife brushed my hair and stabbed into the door. It was just millimetres from my face. I started to tremble. He pulled the knife back out the wood and looked to see if he had got me.

He grinned. 'Next time.'

He closed his eyes again and thrust the knife in my direction. I closed my eyes for the second time and breathed a sigh of relief as I heard it connect with the door behind me. I couldn't breathe, I couldn't cry, I couldn't talk. I just closed my eyes and waited to feel the pain. He missed my face again. He repeated this process four times. Then he just laughed.

I was there in my body, but my mind had left me. It was like I had watched it from above. I never once felt the physical pain when he'd hit me because I was consumed with terror. I was frozen to the spot, watching a film reel and I was in the audience. I caught my breath as the game was over, but I still couldn't move a limb.

He paced the floor again. Silently, just staring straight ahead, then suddenly he turned around quick and ran as if to kick a ball. I knew what was coming and curled up as tight as I could. He caught me in the kidneys as I yelped like a stricken dog. He carried on kicking...over and over again.

Occasionally, I'd jolt back into my body and beg my God to help me. Then I'd jolt back out again to watch.

It went on and on for what seemed like hours. There was no escape.

He'd launch into a sustained attack for perhaps a minute, ninety seconds at the most. A furious onslaught where he would just kick and kick and kick and then he'd stop as quickly as he had started.

He'd pace the floor again then call me all the cunts and slags under the sun.

He changed tact. He was bored with kicking me and decided to use his fists again. He took a handful of my hair. I begged him to stop. He didn't hear. He raised my head and he punched me as hard as he could in the mouth. Something snapped, something popped. I was confused. My mouth was numb, I felt no pain. Why did I have sand in my mouth? Then it dawned on me. It wasn't sand, they were fragments of my front teeth. He'd punched and kicked my front teeth to pieces. I spat them out. I was dazed and confused and this whole thing was surreal. I lifted my tongue to feel where my front teeth had been, to see how much he had left me with. My tongue touched gum, a raw bloody gum. It was a living nightmare; would it ever end? No, he was going to kill me. Then it would all be over. He smirked; he was pleased he was strong enough for me to be spitting out teeth.

Suddenly Devon started to cry and that's when I really did jolt back into my body. I was gripped with horror. I looked up and my blood ran cold; he had heard Devon too. He calmly walked to the bedroom and I tried to stand but my legs were like jelly and I fell back to the floor. I wanted to vomit but the maternal instinct in me was stirring. I had to protect my baby. Out of the dream state I had been in, I was now wide awake and gripped with absolute horror.

There are no words to describe how I felt. Bob walked back through into the passage. He had lifted our little six-month baby out of her cot and never spoke a word. He held her up towards me and grinned a vacant looking grin. He settled the blade of the knife against her delicate beautiful neck and started to pace the passage again. My head raced. I had to do something.

I started to beg, 'Bob, please put the baby back in her cot. This is all my fault; she doesn't need to be part of this.'

Again, he wasn't listening.

'Please, hurt me but not her, please not her.'

He marched into the living room. I crawled on my hands and knees after him. He'd remembered he still had alcohol and settled down into the armchair with a glass in one hand and the baby in the other, the knife resting on his knee. I edged out of the room slowly. It was as if he hadn't even noticed I was there. I quietly edged out of the room, into the passage and crawled out the front door. I knocked on the next-door neighbour. Not too loud that Bob would hear, but loud enough. I prayed that someone would answer.

A little old lady opened the door about two inches wide, obviously scared for her own life. I whispered to her to ring the police.

'I'm a hostage, my boyfriend is going to kill my daughter. Bob, he's called Bob, and he has a knife at my baby's throat.'

The colour drained from her face and she closed the door.

Why had she closed the door? That wasn't in the fucking script! At least tell me you'll call the police; at least tell me you'll help me!

Slowly I walked back into the flat and into the living room. Bob was now standing at the window in our high-rise block of flats. We were four storeys up; he was saying it was all her fault. The baby photo of our beautiful daughter was torn in half on the floor. Time slowed down and the walls disappeared. All I could see was Bob holding my baby at the window and I knew what he was thinking.

The living room door opened wide and the little lady from next door stood there, like an angel sent from God. She was in her nightdress and dressing gown. She took two steps closer to Bob and spoke softly. 'Hello son. Hand the baby back to her mammy, you don't want to do this pet.'

Was she serious? I looked at Bob, I looked at her and back to Bob. He was still trance-like, but something had shifted. There was a different look on his face.

'C'mon Bob, you're a lovely lad, hand the baby back to her mammy, eh? That's it Bob, come on son.'

She was like an apparition, all soothing and calm like a celestial being, acting as an intermediary to this life or death situation.

His pupils started to contract, his face softened, he shrank in size. It was like he had stepped back into his body. He walked over to me and handed Devon back. He walked out of the living room to the bedroom and packed a few things into a holdall. Very calmly he walked out of the flat and pressed the button for the lift. Once the door closed behind him the little old lady told me to close the door. I did and she disappeared into her own flat.

I sat with my baby and the enormity of what had happened hit me. I started to tremble and cry and couldn't stop shaking. I looked at the clock; it was two in the morning. That whole ordeal had lasted six hours. It was the longest night of my life and a night that would change me forever.

The police and the CID arrived along with my dad. I still have no idea how my dad knew, and all I remember from that time is him telling the police in a trembling voice that it was not the first time Bob had attacked me. He just kept repeating those words. I wrote a statement and I'd see them again the following day. They were now looking for a mad man with a survival knife out on the streets of Newcastle. I put some baby things in a bag. I didn't want to go to the hospital. I didn't feel the need, I never did with physical injuries. Hospitals could never fix the mental anguish. It was the internal pain that crippled me. Not the black eyes or burst lips or broken teeth. The darkness that these attacks took me to, could not be bandaged up.

It was now early morning and I was going to my parents' house. Dad was to go first, and the police would take me and the baby, just in case Bob was still hanging around. On the way out the door I ran back for the vodka. All I could think of was that I needed this drink.

I closed the door to my little flat and took my baby to Mam's.

17

Chicken Legs

I woke up in my brother's old bedroom alongside my baby. I had only managed a few hours of sleep. My head was like a video stuck on replay and I couldn't pause it or turn it off.

My body felt like I had been run over by a ten-ton truck. I slowly manoeuvred out of bed and felt nervous as I climbed down the stairs. I was worried about how Mam would react. The long and short of it was that I felt an utter failure.

I walked into the kitchen and Mam was with my nana Mary. Mam looked up and clearly got a shock when she saw the state I was in. She was distressed and jumped up from the table and started cleaning obsessively.

I sat down next to Nana at the kitchen table. She glanced up at me and started hyperventilating, which turned into an asthma attack. She was inconsolable and struggling to breathe, trying desperately to speak. 'Oh Karen, oh pet, I know how that feels.' She turned to my mam. 'Oh God, I know exactly how that feels.' She paused, trying to catch her breath. She held both ears. 'That's why I went deaf.' She broke down, crying even harder. 'Too many hidings,' she kept saying with laboured breath.

Now it was me who started to cry. I cried not because of the pain within me but because my poor nana was in pain. My beating had taken her back to a time she had long forgotten. Her body shook and she had to keep inhaling on her Ventolin. It was a horrible thing to witness. I felt bad for her. I had never seen Nana like this, and I had never heard of her enduring any abuse, but clearly, at some point in her life she had.

Dr Grant from the local surgery came out to assess the damage and as he was writing down what injuries I had, he said, 'You're lucky that there isn't any major trauma to your body. The extent and the number of injuries proved that this assault went on and on and on.'

I just nodded. I didn't have the resources or the inclination to communicate.

Photos were taken and a diagram drawn, pointing out what injuries I had to my face and body. I had a black eye, bruising to my temples, split lips inside and out and three of my teeth were shattered. I had numerous cracked and broken teeth. My ribs were all bruised, as were my arms both inside and outside. My back, above my kidneys, was bruised too and the jeans that I had been wearing left the pattern of the fabric on my legs where I had been repeatedly kicked. Even the seams of the jeans had left an impression on my skin down my outer legs and my shins were almost black.

Next was an emergency visit to the dentist where they did various tests to see if I could keep the teeth that had been broken. The dentist hoped they would not have to be removed. He couldn't guarantee that they would hold over the next weeks or months, but for now he would file them all down, ready to build on to. I would start a course of antibiotics for my gums.

The CID and the police never came back for another statement or to pick up the diagram from the doctor, but they did ring Mam to inform us that Bob had been arrested down in London. He was found at his parents' house, all nicely tucked up in bed and sleeping like a baby.

An hour or so later the phone went again. Mam answered. It was Bob's mum. She was going apeshit on the phone about how she had watched her son being arrested and handcuffed whilst still in his boxer shorts and how she didn't approve of this whatsoever. She was complaining to the wrong woman, that's for sure.

My mam listened intently, tapping her fingers on the phone table.

Eventually she bit. 'Oh, pity for you and Bob. You think that's bad? You fucking think that's bad, you thoughtless cunt? My daughter has been beaten black and fucking blue, held at fucking knifepoint by your precious cunt of a fucking son and had the shit kicked out of her and he has even smashed her teeth.' She hardly stopped to breathe. 'So, don't you fucking dare have the audacity to warrant sympathy from us. He is a fucking disgrace. You're all a fucking disgrace.' There was some more abuse hurled down the phone and then Mam asked, 'How the fuck did he make it to London anyhow?'

Mam was still screaming down the phone, repeating certain bits of what Bob's mam was saying so I could follow what was going on. 'What!? Eric came and picked him up from Newcastle? The snobby bastard didn't think to check on my daughter and grandchild while he was up here, they could have been dead for all he knew.'

Bob's mam was now desperately trying to defuse the situation by saying Eric had driven up to take Bob away from Newcastle to do us a favour.

This played with my thinking. Bob had obviously called his

parents from a phone box in the early hours of the morning and his dad got out of bed to drive the five hours to rescue his son. I couldn't get my head around the fact he wasn't interested in his granddaughter; he didn't have a clue whether she was safe. (I'd long given up thinking he gave a shit about me.)

The resentments would gradually start to build over the coming weeks and turn into festering sores.

I immediately went into no man's land and functioned on autopilot. Everything was hazy and even the handling of my beautiful baby became mechanical. Though it would be much later that I realised what I was doing and why. For now, it was one step at a time.

I stayed at Mam's house for exactly one week, then it was time to go back home. I told Mam I needed some normality and Devon needed routine and her cot. We all needed some structure back. I packed my belongings and picked up my baby to go back home.

My brother insisted to take me, and we agreed that we should rearrange the furniture. He told me things might start to feel better. My sister offered to stay with me until I felt better, but for now I would at least try it on my own.

As I turned the key in the front door, I broke out in a sweat. I started to have flashbacks immediately. I looked at the back of the door and there were four big cuts where the hunter's knife had penetrated around the shape of a head…my head that he had pressed against that very door only last week. It made me realise how close I'd been to dying.

In the bedroom, the chair to my dressing table was slashed to pieces. I hadn't noticed it at the time. I have no recollection of when he had destroyed it, but it showed his utter rage.

As I walked up the passageway different images flashed before my eyes. The horror of that night slot into place of context and time. A disgusting smell nearly overpowered Stephen and me. We presumed it was because I hadn't taken the bins out and they'd sat in the kitchen for a week in the summer heat. Jesus, the smell was horrible. I emptied the bins and Stephen sprayed the place with air freshener. Then we rearranged the entire flat and packed all of Bob's things in black bags and stored them in the cupboard. I had always avoided going out onto the veranda of the flats because I feared heights. But this time I couldn't help myself, I had to take a look. Peering down from this height both scared me and made me realise how lucky my baby was.

After my brother left, I settled Devon in her cot, and climbed into bed to have another restless night's sleep. Sleep deprivation had me permanently exhausted.

Next morning, I woke to the putrid smell and I couldn't understand why it was still there. I had taken the bins out, *what the fuck was it,* I thought to myself. I kept searching to try and locate where the stench was coming from.

I started to look around the flat to find the source, but the phone rang and interrupted the search. It was a man from Probation to inform me that Bob had been bailed and that he was hell-bent on seeing me. This immediately terrified me. Probation was so concerned they rang to deliver the message themselves. I assumed they would have informed the police in Newcastle, yet they never got in touch. Probation also informed me of the date Bob was due back in Newcastle to attend court. They said it would not be a good idea to stay at the flat. It was only weeks away.

Reading between the lines, Probation was telling me that Bob still hadn't calmed down. It meant he was angry and was going to get me. Every little sound I heard made me freeze with terror.

I knocked next door to thank the little old lady who saved us with her calm soothing response, but she wasn't in. I'll try again in a day or two, I thought.

I tried to get on with life, but everything was so different. I couldn't relax, I smoked one cigarette after another, and I'd pace the floor constantly. My gorgeous, perfect baby could have died, and I now struggled to hold her tight. I was trying to make sense. It was the fear, I was gripped by fear, afraid of loving something so much because I feared it would be taken away from me. I simply couldn't contemplate life. I switched off that mother's love to protect myself and for self-preservation, subconsciously thinking that if I didn't love my child so much, no one would harm her.

The bond that bound me to my daughter was somehow severed. An invisible scalpel of hurt had severed my maternal connection. I was terrified to love her again. To me love equalled pain and at this point in my life I could not go through any more pain. Other than fear, I felt nothing. I was numb. I was distracted but random thoughts raced through my head, replaying the same video clips of useless information.

Two days later my brother came back to the flat. 'What the hell is that smell?'

'I've searched every day, Stephen. I don't know, I haven't got a bloody clue.'

The smell seemed to be all over the flat, but we narrowed it down to the kitchen. We pulled out everything and the last thing to be moved was a very large fridge freezer. Behind the back of the fridge we found the offending articles. Rotting away with maggots dropping from the putrid meat was the chicken breasts and chicken legs I had taken out to defrost on that fateful night.

I hadn't put them there. It could only have been Bob.

Disgusted and confounded as to why Bob would hide chicken was beyond me, but we needed to search the rest of the place thoroughly just in case he had hidden anything else. We undertook a search of the flat with a fine-tooth comb. The tin where we kept our bill money had gone. No surprise there, I thought. I found pornographic magazines under the carpet in the bathroom and an itemised phone bill revealed dozens of calls to sex lines. Who was this guy? I reconsidered my sister's offer to stay with me because I just couldn't settle. Bob was clearly unpredictable and unstable.

A few days later the phone rang. It was a familiar voice. It was Bob. I froze. His first words were, 'Did you find the chicken?'

I could almost sense him grinning on the other end of the phone.

'You did that on purpose?'

'Yeah.' He said, all smug.

'Why would you do that? Why?'

'So you would get maggots in the carpet.'

So, he wanted that to happen, I thought to myself. 'But your daughter crawls around that carpet. Your daughter Bob, the baby we made together, your flesh and blood.'

Silence.

I wrestled with the idea of a human being, a father of a baby who spent most of her time on the floor learning how to sit and how to crawl, wanting maggots crawling around our carpet. I couldn't comprehend it. I'd never comprehend it. I needed to end this phone call.

'I...I've got to go,' I stuttered, 'I don't think you're meant to be contacting me.'

I hung up nervously and ran to make sure the front door was locked. There was no remorse in that voice. If anything, he was mocking me and enjoyed the fear in my voice. He had no respect for the authorities, and he had no respect for me or his daughter. That worried me greatly.

Within days Probation also got in touch to remind me that I shouldn't stay in my flat on the day and night of Bob's court case, which would be held soon. My anxiety reached new heights.

This was all new to me and my family. We had no idea how the courts worked. I assumed the police would have been back to keep us informed of all developments and to ask more questions, considering the court date was approaching. The statement I had given that night had been somewhat rushed, as I just wanted to go to Mam's house. I was in shock and initially couldn't remember everything, just bits and pieces of continuous beatings. I sure as hell hadn't told them the extent of the horror we had endured.

I trusted the justice system and the police, but I hated the lack of information about what was going to happen and why I was not being called to court.

I rang Mam and voiced my concerns about the potential risk and why we still hadn't had any information from the police. We were told nothing, given no advice. We went to the police station on Gosforth High Street to say we were concerned for our safety. There was a Newcastle game on and most of the officers were there, so they couldn't even spare one to talk to me. The civilian girl behind the desk called after me as I walked out of the station. 'If you have any trouble, phone the police.'

Sound advice, I'd bear that in mind.

I felt frustrated and rage pushed up from the pit of my stomach to my throat. I noticed a brick lying on the ground. For a few seconds I seriously contemplated throwing it through the station's window. I would be arrested and would be safe at least. It was the first time any rage-like emotion had ever surfaced in me. I was so used to repressing all my feelings that they usually just turned into depression. But now something was definitely bubbling under the surface and it was very disconcerting. I stuffed the feelings back down again and tried to put plans in place.

Mam said I'd have to stay at Nana's the day of the court proceedings, and we would get Uncle Terry to stay at the flat. We were worried Bob would break in, especially as his belongings were still there. Even if me and Devon weren't there he could still hide and wait for us. God knows what he could do if he got in. He'd planned for his daughter to crawl amongst the maggots and held her at the fourth-floor window. He was capable of anything. I didn't want to take any risks.

I don't even think we had a solicitor. It was the duty solicitor who would be acting on my behalf, and we hadn't even met him, but Mam and Grandad wanted to go down to court. She wanted to look at Bob. I was strongly advised to stay as far away as possible and I didn't need to be told twice.

The day arrived and I was staying at Nana's, waiting for news. I wasn't sure what to expect but I realised he was a very dangerous man and very angry with me and our baby. If he at least got some jail, I think I would have relaxed, at least enough to recover from our ordeal. Living in a constant state of fight, flee or freeze was making me sick with worry.

I waited by the phone all day and eventually it rang. It was Mam. She was livid. She had been told to wait in the waiting room and she'd be called when Bob was due before the judge. They had waited in the waiting room for ages when Bob, his lawyer and dad walked by, smirking. He walked free. It had all been over and done with. No one had told Mam.

I couldn't get my head around it as Mam said they had been tricked.

'What? You missed the reading and everything? How?' I cried, realising that we'd never know what Bob had said and why he'd walked after such an attack. 'What happened, what was his sentence?'

Mam had checked with the duty office. He got a suspended sentence and a fine of £200.

'What the fuck! You cannot be serious!' I screamed down the phone.

'And he was made to pay £80 damages to you,' Mam said.

I felt insulted, what I went through was worth £80? The law had disregarded the value of our lives. We were worth nothing. Not that I ever was, but now my baby wasn't, either. It was his father, the rich snobby bastard; he had hired the best fucking barrister money could buy and they'd won. They'd released a thug with a criminal record, just another crime added to the list, and the only deterrent was a fine which was loose change to Bob's parents. How could the courts allow this?

What was the fucking point of being a law-abiding citizen? The law just reiterated everything I thought about myself. I was a common nothing and not worthy of anything. I felt even more shame. I was now a single parent too.

I had never done anything criminal or harmful to anyone, I had never warranted this hand I had been dealt. It didn't seem fair. It wasn't fair. I was screaming inside but no sound would come out. Rage, anger, resentment; it was all there, but I'd repress it and stuff it back down. Like a pressure cooker, the lid had to be tightened even more.

The days drifted by, coming and going in a blur. It felt better having my sister stay with me though I couldn't hold a conversation with her. Apparently (I remember nothing), most nights I would have nightmares and check all the doors and cupboards before going to bed. Looking for the monster that wasn't there. I would wake myself crying or screaming in utter panic. I couldn't eat and I sure as hell couldn't relax. It was impossible.

Two weeks on, Bob's mum rang and asked when Bob could visit Devon. *She's fucking taking the piss, right?* My legs immediately turned to jelly but I had to act quickly. I told a lie and said I was moving to a new house the week after next, and as soon as I had my new telephone number, I would ring her to make some arrangements. I wasn't really moving to a new house, I wished I could have. I would put things in motion to change the phone number to throw them off. Bob's mum asking for visitation rights for her psychopath son! That fucking terrified me.

Within days a letter arrived from Bob's solicitor, saying that he and his parents wanted visitation rights. They didn't deserve visitation rights. They had fucked that up the minute they rescued him from the crime scene. In my opinion Bob lost all rights to visitation when he held his daughter hostage. I was so fucking angry and scared. What if they took me to court with their expensive solicitor and won, what if he was just wanting to see her to kill her? You read about it all the time in the news. Father in jealous rage kills his own child to hurt the mother. No, fuck him. Not over my dead body. He wasn't going to get anywhere near her.

I had no money to go to court, but I could take advantage of *the first 30 minutes free*, and at least see where I stood. I dialled the number and I booked an appointment to see a solicitor.

The following week I went with Mam and Devon to McKeag's Solicitors on Gosforth High Street. I showed them the letter I had received regarding Bob and his parents wanting visitation and told them what happened on 17 July. Because I had more time to process the incident, I gave them a more accurate picture than I had given for the initial statement.

I had photos too, to prove that the assault had gone on for hours. I told the solicitor of Bob holding the knife at Devon's throat in a trance-like state and hovering by the window. I had no real proof that he contemplated throwing her out, but in my heart, I knew that's what he was thinking. I told them about the chicken he left and how he once said to put a pillow over her head when she wouldn't settle. I was now remembering that night in multicolour vision without the missing gaps. The reality hit me hard in that solicitor's office. I genuinely feared for my daughter's life, and my own. They could also contact Probation to verify that they had concerns for our wellbeing, too. I did not want Bob and his parents having any rights. End of.

My solicitor didn't either and quickly drafted a letter that was sent within days to Bob and his parents, stating what I had said and how we would strongly contest the whole idea. Bob's belongings would be handed to a friend of his and he wouldn't have any reason to see me or even be in Newcastle. If he tried, we would issue him with a restraining order.

I was relieved when my phone number got changed, although Mam had phone calls through the night for several years to come. No voice, just breathing sounds, which I found chilling. We heard no more after they received their letter. I imagined Bob's version of events to his parents were quite different to the reality.

My sister stayed for several months and then moved back home.

Another chapter in my fucked-up life had closed and it was time to pick up the pieces of my shattered dreams. We wouldn't see Bob for another nineteen years, although we didn't know that at the time.

The lovely neighbour that had saved the day… well, I never saw her again. I desperately wanted to thank her, convinced she had saved both our lives. I found out her family moved her into a care home so she would feel safe. That saddened me greatly.

18

Al Pacino and Crazy Karen

I still can't remember Devon's first birthday. I couldn't remember many of the months after the fateful night.

I was numb and concerned that I felt this way. The doctor wanted me to try antidepressants. I thought they might make me feel worse, so I opted for therapy instead. I thought a nice counsellor could perhaps help.

Within weeks a brown letter came through the post with a Mental Health logo stamped on the front in bright red print. My mouth fell open when I saw it. *Oh, for fuck's sake, everyone knows I'm a nutter now,* I thought to myself, *even the fucking postman.*

It was bad enough having to go on benefits when my maternity had stopped, and I couldn't function well enough to go back to work but was too embarrassed to apply for sick money. A dole waller, single parent and now this. The letter told me I was to be an outpatient at St Nicholas Hospital. Can you believe that? I had finally made it as an outpatient at the Loony Bin!

For fuck's sake, my parents' prophecies had come true. I had a mental deficiency and was an official loony. Defective and broken, a faulty product, just what everyone had always said, and I hadn't believed them. More fool me, I thought.

This was the start of my journey walking through the revolving doors of different services from the National Health Service, trying to mend my broken head. My heart had been trampled on, yet it was my head that was now being assessed.

I felt nothing, I was numb. I functioned at the lowest level of emotions without hitting the scale of psychopathic. I wasn't happy or sad, scared or angry, high or low. I was void.

I was to be measured for my competence by Dr W. Shepherd, a psychiatrist who worked for the hospital. His rooms were in a new building with a new name, to reduce the stigma of mental health, namely The Collingwood Clinic. It was part of Newcastle's infamous lunatic asylum at St Nicholas Hospital. It was built to treat the outpatients. The name change hadn't made a difference, every fucker knew it was for nutters and I was now a patient there. I had wanted a nice counsellor who perhaps would offer me tea, biscuits and tissues, instead I was deemed more complex and needed a psychiatrist.

Dr Shepherd looked like someone had pissed on her cornflakes that morning and it was going to be a strained hour. She certainly didn't seem old enough and could only be a few years older than me. She stared across her office desk, enjoying the status she had clearly earned as she climbed the ladder in her profession. Ms Shepherd had a bigger chip on her shoulder than I did. She seemed far happier discussing my skinny frame then ever getting to the root of my problems, my demons and non-existent feelings.

'How do you stay so slim Karen?' she'd ask.

'I dunno,' I replied.

'Do you diet?'

'I just forget to eat.'

'What size are you?'

Is this really going to help me? She's only fucking asking these questions because she needs to lose a stone or two herself.

'So how are you feeling?'

'Numb.'

'What does that feel like?'

Is she taking the piss? I feel numb, I feel nothing, it feels like fucking nothing!

'How is your relationship with Devon, are you interacting with her?'

Oh, here we go, she's trying to trick me to see if I'm a shit parent and take Devon away from me. I quickly played the game.

'We are doing so much better and we have both settled down and are adjusting well,' I said.

I was suspicious of everyone. I desperately needed the help as I was constantly depressed, but I was terrified of saying the wrong thing in case I was deemed unfit to care for my baby.

I would tell them what they wanted to hear and after several sessions would tell them they had done a terrific job and I felt much better.

They bought it. Less paperwork for them.

There was talk of dissociation and Post Traumatic Stress Disorder, but this was the 90's and there wasn't much therapy for that kind of thing. Cognitive Behavioural Therapy (CBT) was brand-new and every now and then I would go along for that. I'd have to keep a diary of my actions and work backwards to see the thought processes behind them. I couldn't talk about the incident with Bob and I still had never told anyone about my childhood. I wasn't ready to open the filing cabinet just yet.

The CBT at that time seemed to shed light on how negative I had become, and the odd outbursts of rage had nothing to do with what

I thought angered me. They were misplaced and yet I couldn't seem to go further back in time than the present. Nothing seemed to help, it was like I had just given up, as if I had gone into hibernation to rehabilitate.

My gorgeous baby was dressed beautifully in pink frilly dresses, but I found it hard to interact and hold her close like I once had. I could do all the manual things, but I was emotionally unavailable. I never slept well, and I couldn't eat. I just existed for a time. I couldn't mix with other people and definitely not join in with mother and toddler groups. I was terrified I would stand out and they'd see right through me and know I was just playing at being a mother. I was vacant and uncomfortable, so this had to be avoided at all costs. I would avoid all social engagements. I would have panic attacks in crowded places and couldn't wait to get back home and lock all the doors to feel safe. My world got smaller. The only place I would visit was my parent's house but one day Mam said she was starting to dread it when she saw me walking down her path. I was horrified and felt rejected again. Years later I could see her point as I was constantly depressed and negative, but at that time I was just desperate for love and support. I stopped visiting and became more isolated than ever. I was a recluse.

Devon's second birthday was approaching, and I had to push myself to finally adjust to our life and get some feelings of normality back. I arranged a little party for her and got in touch with friends I hadn't seen in a long time. They started asking me to go out and put the past behind me, but I was wary. It took time and a lot of persuading but eventually I decided I would.

At first my brother would babysit, but that didn't last too long as when I did finally start to go out, I didn't want to go home. I would promise him I'd be back home by 11.30pm but then roll in the following morning. He wasn't too happy after it happened several times in a row. He told me to get a new babysitter.

I don't know why it happened, but I took that first drink and forgot all about my fears, problems and responsibilities and never wanted the night to end. I started drinking at weekends again and the weekends I didn't go out, I'd get drunk and watch videos of gangster movies. I became obsessed with Al Pacino and Robert De Niro. I watched the *Godfather* movies on repeat and concluded that I wanted a gangster, a hard man, to protect me. I wanted to become a gangster's moll. Those guys were violent bastards for sure, but they looked after the honour of their family and especially their wives. They had more money than the average bloke who worked in an office and there was never a dull moment. It seemed more appealing than the law-abiding citizen that I had been. And the more I watched the movies, the more I believed the illusion was the answer.

I searched for my own Al Pacino. Like with a lucky dip, I always got the dud and I ended up with Dean from Elswick, the most deprived place in Newcastle. I was deluded, totally. But he was about the same height as the real Al with olive skin and dark brown eyes, a villain for sure. Close enough, I reasoned. He was from a well-known family that were into a bit of this and a bit of that and I thought to myself, that will do for me. I knew Bob had heard of him and his reputation so there was no way he'd come anywhere near me with Dean on my arm. Off I went into another chaotic relationship. It was dysfunctional, violent, dramatic, fuelled with alcohol and madness. I really had joined the dark side. He was jealous, controlling and a womaniser. Within weeks I had received one of Dean's backhanders. It really was from the back of his hand, in a swift move that left me with a fracture to my cheekbone and a phenomenal black eye. We were lying in bed when I'd obviously said something to upset him. I hadn't seen it coming. It was that quick and unprovoked. I was startled and hurt, but it wasn't uncommon in this neck of the woods, so I just got on with it.

My life was a car crash, a head-on collision. On the flip side, I told myself I had a dad for my daughter and felt he could protect us both. Long gone was the sensible job and the flowers I once received. This was the lower end of the underworld.

He owned a bar with his brother and another well-known character from the north-east and I worked in the pub for them. It was out of the frying pan and into the fire. It was an incredibly rough pub that all the local villains frequented, where men were men and women were men. They had strippers on Sundays and regular brawls. There was the odd shooting as well and it was a scary world to be in.

We would get a phone call in the middle of the night and Dean would disappear with his brothers and friends to see to business, generally tooled up. And yet he kept everything away from our door and that's just how I liked it. It was terrifying at times but exciting too. However, the pitfalls that come with a life like that were immense, he would womanise frequently and backhand me if he thought I'd stepped out of line. It was expected…the norm.

I would often go to work with remnants of a black eye. I would be kept indoors until it started to heal, people just shook their heads and looked away.

Dean wanted a baby, but I wasn't ready. He threw my contraceptives out of the window one day but luckily, I had some hidden. When he found the hidden stash, I got another hiding. Before long I was pregnant and it was déjà vu, the same scenario was happening all over again. He would be out with other women and I was home pregnant, only this time with a three-year-old as well. Mam said I'd made my bed and I had to lie in it. I lived on the adrenalin of chaos which was my staple diet and cigarettes and vodka took over at the weekends.

One night, Dean rolled home at 4am in the morning, high on amphetamines and wanting sex. My baby was due, and I was tired. I got another backhander and a stern warning that if I didn't, he would set fire to me whilst I slept.

It was easier just giving in and hoping the sex wouldn't continue for hours, because, more often than not, it did. The drugs wouldn't let him ejaculate. The sex was painful, and I hated every moment, praying it would be over soon, but it was safer than saying no and falling asleep.

My daughter was born on 9 April 1994. Dean was nowhere to be seen. I got the bus to the hospital and I was in agony. I had been in labour for days, but the hospital kept sending me home saying the baby will come when it's ready. It didn't, the labour kept starting and stopping. By the time I got to the hospital and they put the needle in my arm to induce me and I wanted to push.

It was a very quick birth and a lot of panic as no one was prepared. I had been telling them for days something was not right. My baby had been stuck low down in the birth canal with the cord wrapped tightly around her neck. There were doctors and midwives running all over the place, it was frantic and scary. She wasn't breathing and needed resuscitation for a good while before they finally got her breathing and eventually the colour came into her face.

I was not equipped to be a mother. I don't know if it was because I had been burdened with responsibilities as a child or because I had never been nurtured. Perhaps it was because I lacked the relevant support, but parenthood never came naturally to me. Other people could read their babies' cues and know exactly what to do. I misread mine. Mother Nature was clearly not there for me. I tried everything to soothe my children but struggled immensely.

I was back and forth to the doctors with a baby who continuously cried, had feeding problems and projectile vomited. I couldn't cope and I was clinically diagnosed with post-natal depression. It was another title to my ever-growing list of what was wrong with me. Dean? Well he was rarely there which suited me just fine.

My daughter Sara was in and out of hospital from the beginning. She had problems with her hearing and had continuous ear, nose and throat infections, which brought on bad asthma attacks. Her speech was delayed, and she wouldn't play with other children. She was destructive and had a high pain threshold which meant she was always getting into dangerous situations with regular trips to

A&E. She would close the door on her fingers and one time the door removed a fingernail. She cried for a minute or two then started playing again. I was exhausted, this child never burnt out, she was like a toy running on a car battery and never stopping to take a breath. I was beginning to rely on alcohol more and more to ease the life I had put myself in.

I lived in constant chaos and fear until the night Dean crossed the line. It wasn't the beatings that made me flip. No, I was used to that. He had slept with a friend of mine and told me all the intimate details as we were in bed to hurt, destroy and humiliate me. He left soon after, leaving me to ponder and beg for his love, but I didn't. After heart-wrenching hours of crying and vomiting the last of my stomach lining, I steadily built momentum in an explosion of utter rage. So intense, I frightened even myself.

Fear stopped running my life. I exploded; I had never ever experienced anything so intense.

I got a babysitter to mind the kids while I jumped in a taxi and headed to Dean's bachelor pad. I knocked on the door full of hell. He opened it to a mad woman and slammed it in my face. It was going to take more than that to stop me. I picked up a heavy-duty garden brush that was sitting on his lawn and started to smash it against his living room windows. He came running out the house with my brother, who had been inside along with Dean's cousin. I saw fear in his eyes. He screamed to our Stephen to get his crazy sister away, otherwise he would hurt me.

I laughed when he said that. Didn't he know that no one could possibly hurt me anymore? I was so full of rage that I had no room for fear or logical thought. Every injustice against me had surfaced. All the times I had repressed my anger now bubbled up. Venom, years of fucking venom, oozed from every pore. I had reached my limit of betrayal and Dean was going to pay.

By now the whole street was outside watching the entertainment and my brother was screaming at me to get in his car. I heard one of the neighbours' mutter that I was 'an insane, crazy bitch'.

It didn't bother me, I felt fearless. I didn't care about people, property or the law anymore. In that moment I had entirely lost the plot and as my brother climbed into his car, I put out the rear-view window and his back lights. He quickly sped away without me. I then started on Dean's car and his van with the brush, smashing it into the windows, the mirrors and the lights. Out of breath, I paused and looked up.

Dean and his cousin stood motionless at the door. They were genuinely scared, I could see it in their eyes, and it was the best feeling in the world to watch the victim become the perpetrator. They went back into the house to call the police.

The next-door neighbour put her head out of the window. 'Hey, that's my brush your using!' she shouted.

I snarled at her, 'Well, you'd better come and fucking get it then, eh.'

She shook her head, ducked back inside the window and locked it. This was Elswick. It was a scary, rough neighbourhood and I had taken on one hell of a scary man. We had been on and off for years, but now we were definitely off. I couldn't risk another incident like that. One of us would end up dead.

In the run-up to this night I had been visiting the council and building a case so that I could get a secret house move. I knew the day would come when I would have to leave. I had been keeping photos and dates of my black eyes and had started keeping a diary. Although we lived separately, Dean refused to let me go. I was in the process of getting an injunction, but it was all thrown out when they found out what I had done. The reality of my stupidity quickly brought me back to earth with an enormous bump.

People called me Crazy Karen after that incident and for a short time I wore that like a badge of honour, but the upkeep and pretence wasn't me. I had two little children who needed me. Not that I was a good mother, but I was doing the best I could with what I had.

I have no idea how I didn't get arrested. Dean had obviously said he didn't know who it was that smashed up his property and I stayed batshit crazy for some time. I scared a lot of people that night. I scared myself too. I knew I had enough venom stored inside me to seriously hurt someone, especially if I chose the wrong route and carried on being destructive. I didn't know how to channel this rage that had obviously been buried. It was looking for a way out, to dissipate. It was unnerving to say the least.

My parents were mortified at what I had done. They thought I had lost my mind and wanted to know how I could do such a thing. Why had I been so angry? It wasn't fucking rocket science.

To me it was obvious. I hadn't been born like this. I had felt mistreated for years, too scared to express any anger, unable to express any pain. It clearly accumulated over time and I had reached breaking point. I was insulted that they expected a better conduct. Had they forgot what I had lived through?

The hypocrisy pissed me off.

Deep down the shame and the madness I was carrying, hurt. I was desperate for my mam to love and help me. If she didn't know how, I thought she could try to understand, even a little. Could she not just hold me and tell me I was going to be alright? Tell me not to worry, we all make mistakes. No, she wouldn't condone me, shame me even more, punish me by casting me out and sending Dad round to scold me into righteousness.

I was twenty-seven years old, with two young children, and Dad turned up at my flat, screaming like a mad man in front of the kids. He told me what a disgrace I was and if I ever talk to them again, he was going to burst my fucking lips. He did what he always did in rage, snarling in my face so close the spit would hit my eyes. His face was red with the veins protruding as he held his fist up to my nose. When Dad did this, it was always with pure hate. That's how I felt. Hated. I glanced at my children who were stunned and afraid, frozen to the spot just watching. Some things never change, I thought. I told him to get out of my house.

Within days I bumped into Dean again. It was during the nursery run. Dean had come out of his way from Elswick, knowing that I would be there.

He rolled down the window and shouted in front of all the parents at the school that I was 'a crazy fucking bitch and that even your own mam doesn't like you, she wants nothing to fucking do with you.'

Before I could say anything, he wound the window up and sped off. He had obviously been in touch with my parents.

Embarrassed, I lowered my head and scurried home. This hit a sore spot and I just couldn't shake it off.

19

Fuck the World

My sister and her family now lived above me in the flats and I watched and studied her carefully. She was a great mother, a loving and caring mam, with a loving partner and they were planning their wedding. A wedding! I wanted to be just like that. Normal.

She would go shopping with Mam and I envied what they had. The thing Dean had said had really wounded me. I couldn't stop the rerun careering around in my head.

I saw an old friend of mine at the shops.

'Why do you always look so depressed?' she said. 'Look at you, you're gorgeous. People would kill to have your figure and you always look so smart with your beautiful long blonde hair. What have you got to be so upset about?'

I couldn't see whatever it was that she could see. It made me feel even worse, it made me feel weak and even more broken. All I knew was that, internally, I fucking detested myself. I couldn't get anything right, I never could. Damaged.

I was unworthy, clearly ungrateful, a lousy daughter and mother. My exterior was my mask, my armour hiding my repulsiveness. My outside did not match my inside.

I had always been a hairdresser and took pride in my appearance. But the words that Dean, and now this girl from the shop, said, played heavily on my mind.

Underneath my appearance I was ugly, hideous even. A fraud.

I snapped, *fuck it, fuck it.* I plugged in the clippers, attached a number two guard, and shaved off all my beautiful long blonde hair. I looked at the result in the mirror and felt relieved as a strange calm washed over me. Finally, I looked how I felt. It felt good initially but within days reality hit me, and I was devastated. I looked like I had been released from a concentration camp. Pathetically thin and with shaved hair. Erratic emotions and impulsivity were not a good combination for me. Spurned and rejected, I nursed my wounds in alcohol.

It was a Saturday night and I wallowed in self-pity; suicide became central in my thoughts. My thinking was that my children would be happier and more stable with my sister and her family. The more I drank, the more sense it seemed to make. I downed more vodka whilst writing my suicide notes. Then I burnt some old scribblings and anything I didn't want anyone reading after I was dead. I then swallowed 150 paracetamols. I got very ill very quick. My brother-in-law had come down and opened my front door to investigate where the smell of smoke had come from. I had started being violently sick, so he frantically ran home to call for an ambulance. My poor sister was beside herself, crying and asking why. All I could say was my children would be happier living with her. The paramedics arrived and ushered me into the ambulance. I honestly believed everyone would be happier without the drama that came with me, especially my kids. They deserved better than what I had been providing for them.

I came to in a ward with IV's in both arms. I was informed very sternly that if this antidote did not work or was administered too late, my liver and organs would fail, and I would need a liver transplant. The nurse said, 'And, by the way, you are nowhere near top of the list, so you will probably die.'

'Thanks.'

'Did you get all that?' she said angrily.

'Yes,' I said sheepishly. 'What's all the black stuff on the bed?' I asked.

'That's the charcoal we made you drink.'

Charcoal? Obviously to make me sick and get rid of the toxins.

We sat in silence for a few minutes. I felt the urge to pee. 'Can I go to the toilet?' I asked.

'Yes,' she replied. 'But you can only go to the toilet with a nurse, you're on suicide watch.'

'What? Someone has to be with me when I go to the toilet?'

She stood with her hands on her hips, nodding. Then she stormed off.

Surely that can't be right, I thought. I got out of bed and my legs were like jelly. I went into the toilet and locked the door.

Suddenly I heard a key from the other side open it.

It was a nurse I hadn't seen before. She smiled, looking embarrassed. 'I'm sorry Karen, I have to watch you, you need to leave the door open.'

Jesus fucking Christ, the final indignity. Could it get any worse?

She watched me pee and I sat there for two minutes.

'Is there anything else you need Karen?' she asked, as if it was the most natural thing in the world watching someone pee. 'Do you need to phone anyone?'

I'll be honest, I didn't know who to phone. It was never going to be a great reception. However, the nurse brought the phone to my bed and I dialled Mam. My only real port of call.

My aunty Gina from Dublin answered. *Oh, shit* I thought, *this was really bad for her to come over this quick.*

'Aunty Gina, it's Karen. Yes, I'm okay. Is Mam there?' I felt embarrassed. I crucified myself at the thought of her coming all the way over from Dublin to support her sister in another crisis, caused by me.

Mam came to the phone and said, 'I don't want you ringing this number again.'

Great. Now Mam had disowned me. All I needed.

My heart sank. 'Okay, I'm sorry.' I hung up.

Her voice had sounded defeated. Or was she annoyed that I was still desperately wanting her love? Either way, I was crushed. I wished I'd died.

The tears ran down my cheeks. On the radio, in the background, was a news report that said the singer Prince's new-born son had died.

I felt selfish. That poor family had lost a son and I had two daughters and had just tried to kill myself. The turmoil! Dear God, if you're there, make it stop!

I was in hospital for several days and I was only allowed to leave when all the blood tests came back stable and normal. My only visitors were the psychiatric team and crisis action team. To be fair, they had always been my support in the background. Thank God for the NHS as they had their work cut out with me. I gave them a brief history of what was happening, leading to my overdose, and they were very understanding and helpful. They were going to get me a social worker and I was also referred to the Alcohol Service in Newcastle. They wanted to talk to me about a dependence and intervention course.

All things set in place, I went home and apologised to my sister and thanked her for having my babies. 'Mam's not talking to me.'

'I know,' she replied, 'I've already pointed out to her a mother should have unconditional love for her children, but you know what she's like.'

'I know.' I whispered.

A couple of days later I took Devon to nursery. I was on the defence in case anyone mentioned my shaved head. I could see people were genuinely scared, they'd heard about Dean's windows and my brother's car and now I'd turned up at school with a crew cut.

People were saying it was lovely. They were lying through their teeth. It was fucking awful, but I was growing attached to this new defence technique of being nuts and the world being wary. It was a much better feeling than being terrified all the time. However, Crazy Karen had to be put back in her box as social services were on their way and I needed help, not institutionalization.

20

Organised Chaos

I was a little apprehensive waiting for the social worker and kept looking out the window for what I assumed would be a female. It had been snowing and was freezing that morning. A little stocky bloke arrived, and he looked nothing like I was expecting. He looked like he had just come from university, with that grungy student look. He was all wrapped up in multi-coloured clothes.

He settled down by the fire and sunk into the armchair. He was friendly enough and not as belligerent as I thought he might be after hearing so many bad stories about Social Services. I found him easy to talk to and incredibly helpful, which immediately made the censoring of what I needed to say a whole lot easier.

I told him about the relationship that I had with Dean and how he'd still come by to torment me and I told him what he had said about my mam. I also told him about the backhanders I frequently got, and how he constantly slept around and demeaned me. I briefly mentioned a little about Devon's dad, but I was still unable to go into detail about it, and I explained how my self-esteem had always been lower than a snake's belly.

I talked about how my youngest was in and out of hospital and how I found it all difficult to manage on my own without support. He listened and talked when I stopped. I was genuinely surprised how better I felt when he left. Not the most conventional of social workers, but a good listener and very helpful.

Social services said they could help by providing me a childminder once a week for a couple of hours so that I could get some rest, or just to have a little 'alone time', as they called it. I was also to engage with an organisation named 'Woman's Aid', who would decide on how to move forward without Dean and protect my little family in the future. They said they might be able to help get a quick house move since I could no longer go for an injunction.

Positive framework for growth.

Dean was still tormenting me and adding to my mental deterioration and the welfare of my family, so off we went to a refuge in Byker for weekly visits to learn about red flags and attend self-esteem classes. I was to have specific counselling from their non-profit organisation where someone would come to my house and attempt to break the cycle of abuse.

Newcastle's drug and alcohol service had a lengthy waiting list, which was music to my ears, as it meant I could justify my drinking whilst I was waiting.

My counsellor from Woman's Aid was called Penny Hardman (ironically). She was the support I had been looking for my entire life. She was a tall and thin student-looking woman, who turned out to be a fantastic advocate for women who suffered from domestic violence.

I'd say things like, 'I deserved it Penny, I was miserable, I'm so negative.'

She'd say, 'No one deserves to be beaten Karen, not ever.'

I'd say, 'But he said he had slept with my friend because I was boring in bed.'

She'd say, 'They all say that to justify their actions.'

'My dad told him to knock me out if I caused him problems.'

'Well, what kind of comment is that from a father?'

'I know, I swear it gave him the green light.'

'Most probably, but what we have to do now is build your confidence and self-esteem. We'll teach you how to recognise red flags that you have, no doubt, had in the past ignored.'

This was the first time I truly opened to anyone. She was a godsend and unravelled a lot of the confusion around domestic violence and how there was a pattern. My pattern was that I didn't know any other, it was familiar to me, I'd grown up with it. My core beliefs were that I wasn't worth anything, so the abusers immediately saw the vulnerability in me. Sick attracts the sick. I felt I deserved the harsh life because I had been born bad.

Penny and I worked on changing core beliefs, but it was difficult because they had been ingrained in me since I was a small child. I took a long time to build my strength and gain some confidence because my foundations seemed to be built on sand. I would do good work for a little while, but it would easily be undone. A couple of negative comments came my way, or some gossip would filter through the grapevine about my parents' disappointment in me, and I would be back at square one. However, seeds were planted that would forever be in the background, prodding me that this wasn't the only way to live.

Woman's Aid helped me get a safe house, already kitted out with panic alarms. It was in everybody's best interest to move to a new house and start again. Yet, at the same time I felt very alone.

I wished Penny could have stayed in my life forever as it could have been a real turning point for me, but there were other women she had to go and help. I understood. So, after a year of visiting her every single week, she was gone. Just like that. I missed her immediately and felt alone and fragile again, but at the same time I was looking forward to a new start with just me and my children.

Social services got Sara into a playgroup, so both kids were now in a new school and we all had some stability for a time. A couple of years at least. I never saw my parents during this time and as much as I'd shrug my shoulders and say it didn't bother me, it was always in the background or forefront of my mind, depending on how I was feeling. Nevertheless, I felt as if, for once, I was coping with life in general.

Uncle Terry lived close to my new house and he frequented the local pub. On passing one day, I called in to see him with the kids. I desperately needed the adult company. It seemed so harmless and my intentions were to just kill an hour. He bought me a vodka and coke. What I didn't know was once I took one drink; I wouldn't be able to stop. All common sense and good intentions went out the window. Several hours later I was still there to the amusement of every normal punter. My poor little children were still in tow as we headed back home early evening. They hadn't had their tea or bath for bed. In the morning I promised myself I'd never do that again.

A month later I couldn't help myself and I searched for company so went back to the local pub. This time I got chatting to some of the regulars. It was great fun, before long we were all exchanging phone numbers to meet again the following week. Most of them had done some sentence or other in prison and when I was sober the whole idea scared me. Yet, when I was drinking with them the thrill and the stories made me feel alive. I started feeling accepted by this group and though it wasn't ideal, at least I wasn't alone. I figured that as long as I stayed single, I would be okay. It's only when I got myself into a relationship that things started to go wrong. And so, I went with the flow and my new friends introduced me to a lot of parties and a lot of drugs and a lot of people who had spent time with Her Majesty, at her pleasure. And that was mostly the women.

It was the group culture and once you had been accepted, it was very hard to get out. I got caught up very quickly and got sucked into their world for a time. I went on jail visits and spent time writing jail mail to various convicts that you probably wouldn't poke with a stick in the outside world. But I figured, what harm could it do when they were locked up. The harm was that my associates were incredibly unsavoury characters and unsavoury characters live in unsavoury ways. The chameleon in me adapted quickly to my new surroundings that were not for my highest good and I got mixed up in the madness for a lot longer than I should have done. I never committed any crimes myself as I was too strait-laced for that, but I did keep the parties going for days and days and my nick name of Crazy Karen was back.

I laughed when they called me that, I was a part of something again, I had an identity. However, it wouldn't be long until I would cringe at that very same name.

It became way too reckless and fast for my liking and coming around one morning after a night I couldn't remember, I found one of the locals in my bed. It made me detest who I was becoming. I also realised that they were beginning to take my kindness for weakness, and they were right, I was very weak in comparison, living a way that wasn't me. They were taking advantage of me and my house.

The excitement of only months ago, had turned to fear and fatigue. The scary stories I had once thrived on were now starting to haunt me. I struggled to get my life and the old me back. Once or twice I got home late and they had already let themselves into my house, sitting using my gas and electricity. My house had become their hub. The Valium the doctor had given me for my nerves had all disappeared, stolen. The neighbours were getting sick of the noise. The more fear consumed me, the more my alcohol consumption increased.

I was getting pulled onto a very slippery slope. I was far more vulnerable than I had thought, and no matter how much I tried to hide this vulnerability, people could and would sense it a mile off.

I missed Penny. I missed her badly. I felt alone and lost, trying to fit into a hostile world, gravitating towards anyone who showed some acceptance or kindness, which was always used against me. But as much as I realised it, I couldn't do anything about it. I was doing so much better when Penny had been in my life. I needed a positive influence, good strong role models but they were few and far behind in a pub full of ex-convicts on a shit council estate.

The long-awaited appointment with the drug and alcohol service finally arrived and I thought yes, this is timely, I can leave this world behind and get out of the hole I'd dug myself in.

On the day of my assessment to access the service from Newcastle's Drug and Alcohol team, I dressed to impress, so that they wouldn't think I was a nutter who hung out with nutters and partied most days and nights, even though I did. I thought I needed to look like I had it all under control. A contradiction, I now know.

I turned up at the building and I was clearly overdressed. I wore a business suit and small heels, my hair and makeup set in place. I was ushered into the waiting room when it dawned on me that everyone else looked like they were all homeless. They had surely turned up for a soup kitchen and they had arrived for feeding. Then it registered that they were clients, screaming for their methadone and kicking off with the staff because their fix had been reduced. I hadn't met any real addicts before. One lad had all his tattoos spelt wrong and instead of it reading, *Mam and Dad* across his fingers it read *Bad and Mad.* In fact, it may have been meant to say that. Oh, Christ, what was I doing in this place?

Everyone was arguing and demanding drugs or shaking, spitting and fighting. It was like a scene from *One Flew Over the Cuckoo's Nest* and it was horrific. Me, I looked like I was going for a fucking interview at the tax office. I looked around, I knew I was losing the plot, but surely, I'm not this bad.

I wasn't an alcoholic and besides the glue-sniffing, the odd wrap of speed, an ecstasy and some LSD once, I had never met a real junkie. These were real alcoholics and addicts.

I talked myself out of it. There's been a mistake, I told the staff, my crutch of alcohol is no longer affecting me. These poor fuckers really do need the services and I don't want to be taking up anyone's time. They tried to persuade me to stay but I wasn't having any of it.

'Goodbye,' I waved, as I hurried out of the door checking my purse was still inside my handbag.

For fuck's sake, fifteen months I had waited for that appointment and off I went back home where the phone was already ringing off the hook, my new gang of friends wanted somewhere to sit and drink. A well-adjusted person would have had the courage to say no to this gang and safeguard her boundaries and house. I wasn't capable of that. I didn't know how to set boundaries. I didn't even know I was allowed to set boundaries.

My life and house were being taken over. I did what seemed the easier way out, I moved to a new house instead. No sooner had I unpacked and decorated the new house, that I'd pack again and ask for a house exchange. It became a pattern that would continue for many years. It was an expensive solution to my problems. The correct term is "Addiction geographical" in the world of recovery, meaning running away from yourself and not being able to settle in one place with oneself. I hadn't made the connection that every time I moved to a new house; I took the problem with me. *I* was the problem.

My new house was decorated beautifully, but what an area we now lived in; on the edge of Fawdon. Neighbours fighting in the streets and everyone whizzing around on speed and white lightning. It was clear that I came to view this estate on a quiet day and the residents I had exchanged with must have jumped for joy when I fell into their trap and agreed to the exchange. It was a cross between the Bronx and a gunfight at the OK Corral.

I hadn't seen my parents since the fight with Dean and taking an overdose three years previously. Mam needed an operation on her back, and she had a collapsed lung after surgery. This time she really was sick. No games.

It had been a while since I had seen her, and I was apprehensive walking through the ward in the Freeman Hospital. I got a massive fright when I saw her. She looked ill and frail. She couldn't really respond due to the oxygen mask, but I guess we made up. After a tearful hour I left feeling awful, sad and conflicted.

I did as I had always done when I felt emotional or couldn't explain, or control, my feelings. I drank and drank, and it just kept increasing. A quarter bottle of vodka had turned into a half, which quickly spiralled into a 75cl bottle, and it just kept progressing. It was my comforter and my friend, but then it started to turn on me and became an enemy. I'd walk to the shop saying a mantra to myself; I'm only buying a little bottle, I'm only buying a little bottle, please only buy a little bottle. Then I'd come home with a big bottle. The committee in my head would be arguing and again I would repeat another mantra; I'm only having a few drinks, I'm only having a few. But then I'd wake up and the bottle was empty. Life became a drunken blur and I felt unable to control it.

I was going around in circles and it was making me dizzy. I was becoming more reckless and came round from unconscious states, not knowing where I had been or with whom. My days and nights were merging into hazy confusions of what was real, what was drunk, what was imagined. Did I really do that, or have I dreamt it? Was that a hallucination or had it been a movie?

Is it 4am or 4pm, it's pitch-black and I'm confused? If it's 4pm, I've forgot to pick up my kids from school, if its 4am they will be in bed. Argh, the panic! Every now and then I could reign it in for a few months before it sneaked right back. As I progressed, the reigning-in got smaller and shorter.

I fuelled my alcohol with the insidious chatter of failure. I convinced myself I was a lousy daughter, a lousy partner and a fucking terrible mother.

I always had false hope and told myself that if I got the right house in a better place, I would be happy. If I met the right man, I would be happy. If I learnt how to put the top on the bottle after a couple of drinks, I would enjoy an occasional night out and be happy. I was always trying to fill the hole in my soul. I picked up more work hairdressing to keep me busy, but I was always hung-over. I even went back to college and passed an HEFC in psychology, but my achievements were still not enough.

Sara was still back and forth to the hospital or the doctors' and she was diagnosed with ADHD. She was now eight years old. She was also getting into a lot of trouble at school with frequent phone calls from the headmistress asking me to call in to see her. It got to the point where I didn't want to answer the phone as it was constantly negative. Mam said it was because of my parenting or lack of it.

We were constantly ostracised, me and the children, and it bothered me a lot that Mam could never see the obvious or be kind and supportive. Every holiday we spent on our own. Every Christmas Day we spent alone. My parents spent their Christmas Day with my sister. The constant criticism and continual rejection made me reach for my self-sabotage button. I fed the gossip and the shame and then the self-loathing. Every label I was ever given I became incredibly good at acting out.

The more they criticised me, the more I'd conform to what they were saying. The labels stuck. *You're a failure.* They were right. I was the world champion at failing. *You're a useless cunt.* I'd be up there with the most useless cunts around. *You will never amount to anything.* I was too scared to try anything.

On and on. There was never any recognition for the good, positive things I had done. It was as if nobody noticed anything good that I have achieved.

I'd wind up in a pub, taking drinks off whoever was buying.

There was always somebody buying because they wanted something at the end of it. I thought men were being kind and generous, but they wanted payment in various ways and my esteem was so low I would feel obliged. They would buy me alcohol for sex, and I'd give them sex for alcohol. It became a commodity. I would come too, and be horrified, and it eroded my self-worth a little more. I became vacant and used them as much as they used me, but it ate away at my very being. I would try to scrub away the smell of cheap aftershave and wash away memories of the previous night, but no matter how hard I scrubbed, I couldn't wash the disgust away.

My children were living with a drunken mother who was emotionally unavailable and now mentally very sick. Me, well, I turned into the very people I blamed for my lifestyle and insane choices. I was a victim stuck in anger, blame and self-pity and hurting the people I loved the most.

Sara's dad found out where we lived and wanted to see the two kids. They were excited; it had been a few years since we had seen him. He took them out for the day and the next weekend he had bought them bunk beds at his house so that they would eventually sleep at his at the weekends. It sounded good but his new wife was less than enthusiastic about these new stepchildren and the rot set in soon after.

Within weeks there was tension and Dean was overly stern and demanding that the kids should respect him and his new family better. The kids were just pushing boundaries and were now jealous of their father's step kids. After several weekends it all ended abruptly with a letter under the door saying Dean and his wife did not want to see the children again. They had been deemed too unruly. I wrote a letter back saying that respect was to be earned, not demanded.

Just like that they were gone, and I was left picking up the pieces and consoling two little rejected children.

It didn't matter how many counsellors or psychiatrists I visited over the years looking for an answer, the way I felt never seemed to change. The alcohol was the broken record that just kept on playing on repeat. I knew I had to address it. After a bender that seemed to last for weeks, I thought I better do something about it.

I called the AA helpline and was taken to my very first meeting of Alcoholics Anonymous. The woman who answered the phone said she would come and take me herself. Later that day, she pulled up in a car and drove me to a church. It was in the summertime and I was incredibly aware of how it was still daylight and this church that we were walking into had a sign on the door saying AA.

I was mortified. The first thing I did was hide the sign with my body so no passers-by could see where and what I was attending. It seems peculiar now, when I think about staggering home, falling out of taxis and smashing Dean's windows, that I was more embarrassed about walking into this meeting.

The people were lovely and there were no tambourines or men who lived under bushes dressed in rain macs with long dirty beards. They all were dressed well, and they all seemed happy at finding themselves in sobriety. I liked it, but I was angry about the talk of God, as my god had deserted me every time when I needed him most. However, I thought I'd give it a go. I desperately wanted all the bad things to go away but the thought of never drinking again paralysed me. Who would I be without alcohol? What did I like, and didn't I like? How would I cope in this hostile world without drink?

The things I noticed about stopping drinking was that I immediately became a bore to the people who once thought I was the life and soul of the party. They were the same people that would take advantage of me and my house. I told myself I didn't need alcohol and was getting on with a much more peaceful life.

I concentrated more on the kids and took an interest in their hobbies. Sara was a phenomenal footballer; I had never realised this before now. Devon was an amazing singer. I'd be on the pitch at the weekends and put Devon's name down for every singing competition there was. It was huge progress, but I struggled with feelings and hauntings of the past. Alcohol had numbed my emotions, which now surfaced at high speed. I didn't know how to handle, channel or explore them.

Every time me and my children celebrated, we would involve family. The singing competitions, kids' birthday parties, the football finals, anything and everything. Sadly, it most certainly wasn't reciprocated.

Aunty Gina was over on a visit and I rang to say I'd drop by with the kids, but Mam told me to leave it until another time as they were too tired. However, I had to pass Mam's house to get to mine so thought I'd say a quick hello.

I opened Mam's back door and walked through the kitchen into the living room with a big smile on my face. I hadn't seen Aunty Gina in such a long time, and especially not without a drama. I couldn't wait, more so because I was now sober. As I walked in the room immediately fell silent. The whole family and partners were there, dressed to the nines, ready to leave for a party to which I was clearly not invited. I was so embarrassed, I said a quick hello and said I was just passing and wouldn't keep them waiting. I felt foolish. Rejected again, my stomach knotted, and I felt quite faint. Hurt and fragile, I hurried out the door. Crushed. The inner conflict had started; why, why had they done that, why are we never included?

They had lied, bare faced lied to me and I felt stupid. It was clear as day that they just didn't want to associate with me or my family. As I was walking home, the Number 30 bus was passed, and all the family were in there, waving out at me. I waved back as if I didn't care. Two hundred yards later I walked straight into the off-licence and bought a bottle of vodka. It was like putting two fingers up to the family.

I had been sober just a few months; I had felt great. Now I felt like shit. I couldn't deal with these sharp and erratic feelings cutting into my soul like broken glass, it had to be numbed and the only way I knew how was with alcohol. Hello, my old reliable friend, let's get numb together.

It would take another four years before I made it back to AA.

Back on the fucking merry-go-round. Round and round.

21

My name is Karen and I'm an alcoholic

I was starting to become a drunken bum, a nuisance, a train wreck. Every time I drank, I was getting myself into trouble. I was vocal and cheeky and had misdirected anger coming out of me at all angles.

It was getting more dangerous; I was becoming reckless. Outbursts of rage resulted in me one night punching my friend's partner in the face and getting arrested for drunk and disorderly behaviour. To be fair, he was a shit and deserved it, but who was I to be judging anyone? I'm ashamed to say my children witnessed the whole thing and were terrified they would never see me again. I was thrown into a cell in Pilgrim Street Police Station. The saddest thing about the whole ordeal was that when I was released at 5am, the thing I worried about most was whether I had any vodka left at home.

I knew at the time my friend had taken the kids to hers for the night but still, it was the alcohol I worried about. My whole life revolved around alcohol. I would wake up thinking about it and fall unconscious drinking it. My weekend drinking was now most nights and sometimes days depending on the circumstances.

Christmases and social gatherings were ruined by my drunken behaviour. Ironically, I now did give my parents something to blame me for. I tried desperately on my own to not drink but I just couldn't do it. I had good intentions to stay sensible too, but it all went right out the window as soon as I'd consumed the liquid that was now starting to ravish my insides.

My liver was getting poorly. I'd itch like crazy and the restless legs and flashbacks would keep me awake for hours. I'd sweat and shake and vomit. My eyes were turning yellow and I had become ill with alcohol poisoning.

The well-meaning drug and alcohol services didn't work for me. I couldn't control my intake, so drink diaries and the acupuncture, as nice as it was, were never going to help. Though I tried them all, especially all the easier and softer options, it was back to AA I had to go. There was something in there that worked and there is no better example than seeing a person who walked the same walk, now sober and happy. So back I went after four years of a very long drunken spree.

It wasn't easy, every coping device I had used to protect me from the world had to be undone and that was frightening. I had to talk in front of strangers and cringed at the sound of my own voice. I stuttered with nerves and the fear of humiliation and sounding silly used to cripple me. I had never realised how afraid of the world I was until there was nothing left to hide behind. I lived in those meetings, terrified I'd go back on the booze if I didn't attend them.

I was relieved I wasn't the only person on the planet who had found themselves in terrible places mentally, physically and spiritually due to alcohol. We all seemed to feel the same shame and remorse and we all drank to change how we felt. Not for the social aspect but the mere fact we felt empty and scared until we filled our stomachs with the poison that was now ruining our lives and our family's peace of mind.

I had found my tribe.

Within months I was physically feeling better, my nerves were improving, and I met a nice guy named Cliff that kept me wanting more. Everybody liked him. He was charming and funny and although I was advised it wouldn't be in my best interest so early in recovery, I went ahead anyway and started dating him.

He made my little family laugh, he was quick-witted and hilariously funny, throwing the kids around and putting them on his shoulders and I remember thanking my new, sober, God as I thought I was being rewarded for cleaning up my life.

I was sober for ten months, the longest I had ever gone in my life without drugs or a drink. For the first time, my children had a mother who was present and not distracted or intoxicated. This was the first real relationship I'd been involved in since Sara's dad, Dean. I was becoming normal like the rest of the world and not afraid to hold my head high. I was getting some self-respect back and was growing in confidence. And there was new a man who seemed to think the world of me.

We had only been dating several months when Cliff came to visit one afternoon. I had noticed that his eyes looked different, but I couldn't put my finger on why. I also thought I could smell drink on his breath. I tackled him about it, and he said I was imagining it. He couldn't look me in the eyes, he was definitely shifty and hiding something. Within days I had convinced myself he was cheating.

The mind games, the paranoia and the lying were all back, and so was my self-pity, the defect about myself I despised the most.

It turned out he wasn't cheating at all, trust me to have assumed that first. Not cheating but drinking and using heroin and I found out in the most brutal way imaginable. This man changed entirely when under the influence of drink and drugs and went from a charming, caring, funny man to an untameable animal.

The kids were sleeping out the night I was attacked. I didn't recognise him; his whole demeanour had changed. I was so scared when he turned up with some drink, that I asked for a drink too. I thought it would calm him down. His entire personality had changed. I tried to get him out the house and tried to lighten the mood by suggesting we went down the High Street. He agreed. In my head I thought that I will have this little booze blowout while I'm in this predicament and then go to AA tomorrow and get back on the wagon. Make good of an awkward situation, job done.

As soon as we got to the pub, I ordered a wine for me and a pint for him. He drank it fast and was restless and irritable which made me even more nervous. Next round I wanted a faster hit so ordered a double vodka. This person who had been so funny and so comforting was now a misogynist, telling me how all woman were secretly slags just like his own mother had been and generally disrespecting me and any woman close by. He treated me like he hated me and kept telling me to go and dance with someone while he sat with a group of men. I wanted to go back home; it was embarrassing. He insulted the bouncers, so they threw us out. Then he insulted the taxi driver, so again we got thrown out of the cab. He directed his anger back at me, as well as people we passed in the street. He saved his worse insults for the odd girl we passed. Women were dirty whores. He spat at them. I was confused watching this side to a man I hadn't witnessed before. In the end I'd had enough and ran home on my own.

He turned up at my house. I had locked the door hoping he would have gone home. He smashed the small window to the kitchen, broke in and launched into a frenzied attack. He beat me to the floor then straddled me while he banged my head on the concrete tiles.

'Do you know why I was in jail?'

I shook my head. 'No.'

'Do you, do you know why I was in jail, you fucking slag?'

'Burglary,' I whispered between the tears. That's what he had told me.

He laughed, shook his head and then started undoing his trousers. I can honestly say Crazy Karen fought for her life that night. Although he was powerfully strong, I just knew I couldn't stop fighting back. With every ounce of my being I wrestled to get away from being underneath him. I made it incredibly hard for him to hold me down with one hand while undoing the zip to his pants with the other. Every time I almost crawled from beneath him, his arms would hold me back down again. I was screaming for someone to help and was becoming exhausted trying to get him off me. He grabbed me by the throat and started squeezing tight. Oh my God, this is where he murders me, I thought. My eyes felt like they were bulging, I couldn't take a breath and my head and face seemed to be inflating like a balloon. I couldn't hold on any longer, fuck it, he's won. I will just give in. I relaxed, waiting to fall unconscious. Suddenly the police popped their head through the kitchen window that he had smashed, and he immediately changed his demeanour again.

In a calm voice, as if nothing had happened, he said, 'What's the matter officer?'

He was arrested and taken away. The police told me I'd have to make a statement the following day. Shell-shocked and confused, I called a friend to put me up for the night. Upon awakening I couldn't open one of my eyes. The blood vessels in my face had all ruptured where he had tried to strangle me. The scene in the mirror made me cry and it felt like I had fractured ribs. I refused to go to the hospital, more vodka would numb the pain.

When the police came back the following morning, they asked me what I knew about him. I wasn't sure what they were getting at. I said I felt sorry for him as he seemed to have had a hard time when growing up. His mam liked men and parties and he was now in recovery and he was trying to get well but had relapsed. The officer sat down, took a long breath and then asked, 'Do you know why he was in prison?'

'Yes, burglary,' I replied.

He looked confused. He obviously saw something was amiss when he looked into the paperwork he was holding. 'Okay, I need to call the office.' He didn't elaborate, went out to his car and was there for a long time before he came back and spoke again. 'Did you know Cliff was still on licence? Do you want to press charges?'

I paused for a long time as I didn't know what this meant or what to do. I asked him what would happen if I pressed charges.

'He would have to go back to prison to complete his original sentence and probably have time added on for this new charge.'

The thought of sending someone to prison whilst relapsing seemed a rather large burden for me to carry. I said I wouldn't press charges, on the condition he would leave me alone, not come anywhere near me. I had no idea of the extent of his criminal history and would have made a different decision had I been warned and informed. Not being warned, because of legal implications and data protection, left me and my family vulnerable.

They said someone would be in touch.

A few days later social services came to my house and said they wanted a chat. They wanted to know what had happened. I still hadn't pieced it together. As usual I swept the finer details under the carpet. Social services couldn't tell me anything other than me and my children were in danger.

'What?'

I begged them to tell me why, but they couldn't, due to data protection. Naively I asked the social workers if they had the right guy as he had been so affectionate and fun and charming until he drank or used. They said these sorts of men were experts at what they do and homed in on vulnerable people, especially single parents.

'What sort of men?' I asked.

They wouldn't tell me specifics, but I was beginning to get the picture. Oh my God! I had obviously been dating some kind of monster, possibly even a paedophile, and introduced him to my children. I brought him home and welcomed him into our lives. God damn it, hundreds of people frequent these recovery rooms and there are billions of men in this world and yet everyone I get with is worse than the last. What are the chances of that? Is that unlucky? Or do I choose exceptionally bad people?

I had relapsed big fucking style and this time was the worst my drinking had ever been. I couldn't get the message from social services out of my head. I constantly played the rerun of what they had told me. Then I would play the recall of the last ten months to try and figure out if I had missed any signs of the danger we were now facing. I analysed every day up until that moment, wondering whether he was just being kind to my kids or whether he was manipulating them for other reasons. It didn't bear thinking about. What was it that social services weren't telling me? I needed to know. I was desperate to know, but how?

Intoxicated and not thinking straight I decided to try and get hold of Tommy. I needed help. This Cliff guy bailed without charge and was now trying to get in touch with me and sending cards through the post to the kids. I needed to find out the whole story. Knowledge is power. I scrolled through the phone book and found Tommy's business listed. There was a mobile number attached. I sent a text to say I was looking for Tommy and could he please get in touch.

The next night my mobile rang, I answered it to a very loud, familiar voice. 'Hallow, who's this looking for me?'

'Tommy, it's Karen. I'm in trouble.'

It was 2002. I hadn't seen Tommy in over fifteen years. I was thirty-five years old, had two children, aged eight and eleven, and I was in the middle of a relapse, terrified of what and who this Cliff person was.

Tommy came around that night and I told him my predicament over a shared bottle of vodka. I immediately remembered why I had not seen him for all these years. He was loud and overbearing and yet I knew he would be able to help me. He knew everyone in Newcastle. We caught up on the years in between. He had been living in Thailand for a time and had two children, but that relationship had ended. I didn't want a relationship with Tommy, I just needed help. I didn't pull the wool over his eyes or lead him on. I put him in the picture from the start. My track record of relationships was my Achilles heel, so it was the last thing I needed. He left to go home, and I went to bed, pleased I had ended our relationship back when I was nineteen. No regrets in that department. He was a good guy but definitely not for me. It was exhausting being around someone that was so loud and full-on, and I crawled into bed absolutely drained. But it was also reassuring that I knew he wasn't a wrong un' or handy with his hands towards woman.

The next day I woke up to a knock at the door.

Tommy was standing there.

'Okay,' he said. 'So, you say this guy is originally from Newton Aycliffe, well let's start there. Jump in.'

I did as requested.

The next few days were the same routine. He'd turn up; we would drive to Newton Aycliffe to the town library and check the archives, looking to see what we could find. But we were drawing blanks and I was starting to get sick of the detective work, day in and day out, not quite knowing if we were doing it right, or if we would even find out anything. Then we struck gold. A week in and playing investigators, the computer screen of the Archives department suddenly turned up something interesting… his name, Cliff Steeple.

I read a paragraph from the archived newspaper.

Man convicted in 1997 for three offences of rape, attempted rape, and attempted indecent assault on a 16-year-old. Clifford Steeple aged 33 of Newton Aycliffe, Durham.

My heart started pounding in my chest, 'Jesus fucking Christ.' He had not been in prison for burglary, he had been in prison for rape, he was a sex offender, a rapist.

The drive back to Newcastle was the longest car journey of my life. As the car pulled to a stop outside my house, my neighbour Jan from across the street came running. 'Karen, Karen have you seen today's *Chronicle*?'

She was holding it in her hand. On the front page was a picture of the man who had been at my house to see Cliff. It was Cliff's best friend. It said he had been in prison for ten years for rape at gunpoint. I swear the blood in my body froze as I leaned up against the car for support. They had clearly met inside. He had been in my house more times over the last few months than my own family had. I was absolutely gobsmacked. Jan and Tommy could see that my legs were about to give way and helped me into the house. Jan made me a cup of strong tea.

I have no idea why I was so gullible, believing people and seeing the good in the very, very bad. It could have been Ted Bundy and I still would have believed him if he had said he had been sent to prison for unpaid motoring fines. My natural defences for danger did not work whatsoever. The realisation of what could have happened to me and my children made me physically sick and I spewed my cup of tea into the sink as soon as I had finished the last drop.

I knew I had to get sober again. I knew I needed the meetings of recovery but while Cliff was still frequenting them I couldn't. It was too dangerous. Tommy said to leave it all with him and it would be sorted. For years I had blamed my God for giving me this life, yet I suddenly realised that I wasn't so unlucky. I was incredible lucky really because some of the people I had associated with could have done me serious harm and destroyed both me and my family. And yet someone or something had always saved us in the nick of time. My trusting of bad people had been familiar, but it didn't have to be like this.

Tommy came back within days saying Cliff was no longer living in Newcastle. He said he had left voluntary and then smiled, 'But in a bit of a hurry.'

He said I was now safe, and I could go back to the meetings I so desperately needed. There was no way Cliff would come back to Newcastle. It was a relief.

No one believed the story about Cliff as he was so charming when not pinning down women, trying to rape them. It didn't matter. I knew the truth and that's what mattered. Even my parents thought I had made up the story to warrant my relapse. Disowned for another few years.

My drinking had progressed to everyday drinking. A full-blown alcoholic.

I sheepishly went back into recovery and got a sponsor; this time I did everything I was told. My life depended on it.

It's strange. I had seen so many psychiatrists and tried so much therapy over the years and what started changing my life was sitting with a bunch of drunks trying to get well. Ironic. The best therapist in the world, someone who spotted all my flaws, as well as all my positives, turned out to be a middle-aged cleaner from Wallsend. She taught me to become honest and that my car crash life could actually help other women. I found this hard to believe at first, as I was embarrassed about the way I had lived my life. She said if I could turn my life around after going through what I had gone through, so could other people. She loved me better, she was the first person who believed in me. My sponsor Iris, my AA teacher.

I started to want a new way of living, I wanted to get well and have choices, I wanted to face my past head on and turn negatives into positives. I was ready to be redeemed, I had surrendered to alcoholism.

Within three months of attending AA meetings and abstaining from alcohol, it was my turn to tell my story of alcoholism and how my life had changed now I was no longer a drunk or using drugs. I was terrified.

Everything was mixed up and messy and I didn't know where to start. How could I tell strangers where my alcohol and bad choices had taken me? How could I look people in the eyes and say how I would literally use my body as a commodity for another high, a drink or a scrap of validation? How could I possibly put it all into chronological order when it was all mixed up and fragmented? How?

A woman told me to go and pray and ask God for the right words, the strength and the courage.

I hid in the toilet, praying madly, 'Dear God, I know I've made a mess of my entire life but please help me to stay sober and let me be able to help another person by telling my story. I pray, I will be honest, and I beg you not to let me faint through fear. Please give me the courage to tell my story truthfully and offer some hope to the still sick and suffering. Amen.'

Everyone was ready, it was a packed little room in the middle of Newcastle, I couldn't stop shaking and then I was introduced to tell my experience of addiction.

'Holy fucking shit,' I whispered under my breath. 'Don't desert me God, don't you dare.'

Then I spoke up. 'My name is Karen and I'm an alcoholic.'

Wow, it really hit me that I was a real alcoholic. I wasn't homeless or lived in the Exhibition Park, I wasn't a man, like the stereotypical version I had of alcoholism, but when I drank, I couldn't stop, and I would get myself into incredibly dangerous situations. Crazy Karen was just my ego hiding behind my fears and insecurities.

I started by saying I had grown up surrounded by alcohol and violence and how I escaped the misery by losing myself in fantasy and then later in glue-sniffing. I told the assembled group about my first taste of alcohol, aged five. Then I told of my first real experience of losing myself to alcohol and the way it made me feel aged eighteen, at my birthday party, and how I had chased that very first illusion ever since. I told how I went from one sick relationship to the next and how my level of drinking just kept progressing until I had become physically and mentally ill. I told how I got arrested and my poor children thought I was going to prison and how I had never considered their feelings. How I would come to and have no idea how I had got to wherever it was I was. How the very thing that was causing this horrible life seemed also to be the very solution, like being on a hamster's wheel and not knowing how to get off. How that wheel went round and round for seventeen years and how it affected my stinking thinking and mere existence. How I had been in and out of hospital for self-harm and suicide attempts and tried every therapy known to man to cure this insidious illness and nothing had ever worked. Nothing.

I finished by how I thought my God had deserted me through every single beating or violation that I had ever had, but in reality, that I had been saved. I should have died. I cried and said that I realised I had been given a second chance at this thing called life and wanted a better future for my kids. More than anything, I did not want my children to be scapegoated and blamed for my failings as I had been with my own parents. I wanted them unburdened and free to live their own lives without being shackled to my past. I ended my story by saying since I had started attending AA, I had become three months sober, without a drink or drug or man. I took a huge breath and looked out at the people who had been listening.

I was amazed by the reception. People were crying and thanking me, said it gave a lot of people hope, especially women, that they could finally overcome their trials and tribulations and change too. A case of if I could change anyone could. Amen to that.

It was a fantastic feeling to be free.

I felt liberated and the world was now my oyster. I bounced all the way home with the biggest spring in my step I'd ever had.

Tommy was getting way too comfortable saving me and thinking he knew best on everything. I would be eternally grateful for the help he gave me, but he wanted more and was now not hearing me.

Within weeks of finding out about Cliff's crime, Tommy turned up at my house with £200 worth of flowers, a Gucci watch and a diamond ring worth three grand! I knew all the prices because he had deliberately left the price tag on them all. The gifts were endless, but it was a strange concept. Not too long back I could be bought for a couple of vodkas and cokes. Now I was wearing Gucci but the inside of me still felt conflicted and definitely not worthy. I also felt obliged to start a relationship that I didn't want. I knew Tommy would never physically hurt me like the others, but I also knew he was incredible controlling, to the point where he was becoming very jealous of the time I spent with the other alcoholics in recovery.

I began to wonder if I could stay in a loveless relationship but appreciate the fact it was safe, if I could again stuff my feelings down and just be grateful for what I had.

Tommy offered me security, there was no doubt about it. He would give me and my children a better way of living from the poverty and misery we had experienced, but there would always be something missing.

It felt like a trade-off. I get sober and we'd live more comfortably but I'd have every decision made for me. It was stifling, but far better than what we had lived through. The gold, the diamonds, the gifts made me look incredibly selfish, I felt bought and captured and controlled, but without all the badness that came with my other ex-partners. I had hidden my feelings my entire life and I would have to do the same again but was that so bad? I just couldn't bring myself to hurt him.

I would settle. I made the decision to settle down with Tommy.

Besides, he refused to go away.

22

Twelve Steps

I fell pregnant and it was a shock. My body had been so ill because of alcohol that everyone was surprised, even the doctors. Seriously, I must be the most fertile person on the fucking planet. Ironic that Mary Poppins I'm not and yet I immediately fall pregnant at the drop of a hat, or knickers, depending on how you want to view it.

I thought back to the time Devon was born and how it had gone so terribly wrong. This time I wanted to put it all right. I wanted to be a good mam from the start and enjoy a baby, show it off to the world instead of panicking and keeping it quiet in case I got a beating.

I bought every book possible and bought everything my children had never had. There were no second-hand buggies this time, it was all brand new. Tommy insisted and was generous to a tee. One kind lady dropped a bag of beautiful clothes at the door and Tommy shook his head. 'I appreciate the gesture and kindness, but my baby will be wearing brand-new clothes, thank you very much.'

I was approaching twelve months of sobriety but missed my sister and her children immensely. We had been so close. I think she thought she had lost me to AA because she kept herself and my nephews away. When I did see her, she was abrupt and distant. It didn't make sense. I thought she would be pleased, delighted with the new me, a burden no more, not needing to be rescued and saved.

I was constantly asking if I could come to see her, but she always said she was busy. She moved house, even further away, and it was this that forced me to learn how to drive just in case one day she relented and invited me to her new house. She had been like my mother when our own mother disowned me. I grieved for the loss of my sister; genuine, gut-wrenching grief. This was the hardest emotion I had ever felt whilst in recovery for alcohol. Eventually I realised she wasn't coming back, I had to let go.

I was asked to tell my story at a convention along with a dozen others and asked if my mam wanted to come with me. I had been making amendments and working through the twelve steps of recovery and realised how much of a burden and worry I must have been to my family. The 12-steps of recovery was a plan of action for living, it felt like a satellite navigation for life. It was a framework for living, an honest way of being. It is a spiritual and moral compass to stay accountable and become responsible for one's sobriety and one's life. One of the twelve steps is making amends to those you harmed during active addiction. I had many, but typically my children and family, so I wrote heartfelt letters and visited them to apologise for my part in my journey into madness.

My sister, on receiving my apology, later text me to say she missed the old me. This confused me and made me wonder if I really had been as bad as I was saying. I said to my teenage daughter, 'You see, I couldn't have been that bad a drunk. Look, she misses the old me.'

Devon responded with a shrug of her shoulders, 'Easy for her to say, she didn't have to wake up each morning and find you comatose on the floor or find you after another suicide attempt, wondering if you were dead.'

Her response brought me down to earth with a bump.

The more sober I was becoming, the more normal my life looked but the more dysfunctional my own family and past stood out. I was learning to set boundaries so people couldn't take advantage of my kindness anymore. Although I had been a drunk, I had become everyone's babysitter or entertainment host. Now I was saying no, and this upset the applecart somewhat. It was strange as I thought as a family it would bring us all closer together. Instead it only highlighted the defects that were always there, and these were incredibly painful to see with bright eyes and no rose-tinted glasses.

My brother was getting married and it was to be a huge wedding. Two days before the big day Mam summoned us all around her bed again. She was poorly and told us the doctors had found polyps on her bowel and when we asked what this meant, she said cancer. Suddenly, the past rushed through my mind and I could see a pattern. Every time the family's attention was diverted to something other than Mam; she would hit us all with some terrible news of impending death. I suddenly saw clearly how all Mam's illnesses had never materialised. The many, many times we were terrified of our mam dying a horrible death was quite disturbing. We had been traumatised as kids around her bed. There had been a list of illnesses like the hysterectomy that never happened and cancer of the stomach that had disappeared. Or the MS (Multiple Sclerosis), a condition that Mam said would affect her brain and have her end up in a wheelchair. Some illnesses didn't have a name and they had just mysteriously vanished.

Apart from the operation she'd had on her back, nothing else had been official. I watched a movie one night which struck a chord. I looked up 'Munchausen syndrome', a factitious mental disorder in which a person repeatedly and deliberately acts as if they are very sick, to get attention. Wow. Another penny-dropping moment.

Things I'd never noticed in the past were suddenly obvious to me now.

My daughter, Erin, was born on 19 March 2005 and it honestly felt like a real miracle. God had given me a gift; I hadn't felt like I had earned it but made damn sure I would get it right this time. I was a good mam and worked hard to nurture my child. I followed her cues and embraced motherhood. The following month I turned one year sober and in May I took to the stage at the Royal Station Hotel to tell my story of alcoholism. My mother was in the huge crowd of several hundred people and the shock of every one of us sitting on the stage with similar stories made her cry.

She apologised for not realising that I hadn't done any of the stuff to intentionally hurt anyone. I had a disease, that of alcoholism and once alcohol entered my system all bets were off.

I wasn't the only person with this disease and I sure as hell was not going to be the last.

This was the closest and the most intimate time we had ever had as mother and daughter. It was to be short-lived as my sister wasn't too happy about this new arrangement. Her marriage of ten years had ended, which no one had seen coming. She had started to develop her own drinking and eating problems. Mam was quick to the rescue and moved my sister into hers for a brief time, but it had been a special time in my life with my mam. My favourite memory, the only positive memory if I'm honest.

Tommy was taking me out to dinner. It was December, my birthday and he was wearing a suit. Oh God, I just had a feeling I knew what he was going to do. I think he saw me growing in sobriety and didn't like seeing me flourish too much. During the meal he got down on his knee and asked me to marry him. The whole restaurant was watching, how could I say no? It would break his heart. The truth is, we still lived a very superficial life. I had never met any of his staff or been invited to any work-related events. I wasn't even allowed to meet his children. His mam still received all his mail and there was no loving affection in our relationship. It was built on beautiful gifts and me looking glamourous on his arm. There was no intimacy or deep conversations, or anything that looked remotely like a normal relationship.

Yet, I felt I owed him. He had helped me get rid of Cliff and have a decent quality of living. Surely it wouldn't hurt to marry the guy and make him feel happy?

I looked up from the table and the whole restaurant was waiting for me to reply. I hesitantly said yes but I knew it wasn't right. He arranged everything...the wedding would take place in four months' time.

We were to be married in Jamaica with just my children as witnesses.

The destination was the stuff of dreams. I couldn't believe where I had come from, sitting in this beautiful, luxurious place. Tommy knew I had doubts as he said I could change my mind right up until the day. I figured I would finally find the courage to say no. And yet I couldn't do it, I couldn't hurt him. The truth is we were more like brother and sister. We had rescued each other. I hadn't realised at the time that Tommy had an addiction to cocaine and amphetamines, and he was losing his very successful business to drugs. I also hadn't realised that as a child he had been sent to stay at his aunt's on numerous occasions due to his own father's drinking. I also think on some level by rescuing me, he was rescuing his mum.

As I got sober, he eventually got into a recovery programme of his own to abstain from all mind-altering substances, including alcohol.

The day of the wedding approached, and I still couldn't find the courage to call it off. I justified it to myself by thinking it wasn't a real marriage, but a dress rehearsal in another country. There were no celebrations or gifts or family coming together and that suited me just fine. A rehearsal, that sat better in my thinking.

I must admit, we looked the part against the backdrop of the beautiful turquoise sea and white sands. The photos could have been displayed in a magazine. They looked beautiful and they say the camera never lies. Trust me, it lied.

The ceremony was just me and Tommy and my three children. Tommy's other children apparently had other plans. I never knew if that was Tommy's decision or his ex-partner's decision.

I felt like a fraud taking my vows, the only bit I had enjoyed was dressing up for the part. I had an uncomfortable feeling that I was signing myself away and I just couldn't shake it off.

I spent the next forty-eight hours with food poisoning, which really was a bad omen. As I was crying into the toilet, I feared this was the start of my punishment.

It was strange returning home, it hadn't felt real and it was still not common knowledge, which probably suited me more than Tommy.

I had a feeling that Tommy would become even more controlling and that is exactly what happened.

The minute that ring was on my finger and anyone even spoke to me he intervened to inform them that I was his wife. Yet nothing at home had changed. I still never visited his business and his mail still went to his mam's. The children and families were still kept apart. Nothing ever made real sense. I'd sleep in the bed next to our daughter and he slept downstairs on the settee. I couldn't sleep with someone that I could neither communicate with, nor find attractive, now I was no longer intoxicated. Intimacy starts with connection and a liking of minds and soul, and no matter how hard I tried it just wasn't there. Two broken people, pretending to the world that we were like everyone else. Normal.

Besides, now he had the title of husband, he became incredibly cold and authoritative, dictating and talking over me and for me. He was demanding and shrewd and it was suffocating.

The old memory of when I was eighteen returned. Once Tommy thought he had me, he no longer felt he had to try. We both had no real skills to make it work, trying to fit into what society deems the norm. We kept up the charade for eight months, and then I felt I couldn't kid myself any longer. I had shrunk to a size 6 in clothes and weighed just 7 stone 10 pounds when I used to be 9 and a half. I was becoming invisible both metaphorically and physically.

Tired of the lie, I asked him to leave. He would always be my friend, but romantically it was time to face facts. I needed time alone to discover who I was as a person. All through my life I had pretended to be something I wasn't. I had no idea who Karen was. It was time to conquer my fears and find me. Alone. I felt guilty, I hadn't wanted to hurt him, but I was hurting myself. I felt guilty for a long, long time, right up until I remembered he pursued me whilst I was a vulnerable, drunk and self-harming. I realised then that in the same position I would not have pursued someone so unstable. It lessened my burden.

One night around 6pm the phone rang. It was my sister. 'Karen, what's Cliff's surname?'

'Steeple, why?'

'Well, you had better go and put the news on.'

I quickly changed the channel and there, on the national news was Cliff's face plastered across the screen.

The anchor was reading from his autocue.

'Clifford Steeple, a serial rapist attacked again after he was let out of prison early…'

I covered my mouth with my hand. They went across to a policeman and a microphone was thrust into his face. 'He was a brutal rapist; it was the most harrowing case I've worked on in sixteen years…'

What horrified me the most was when the anchor read out the details and said how Cliff had pinned this woman down by the throat before sexually assaulting her, and had asked her, 'Do you know why I was in prison?'

It immediately jolted my - now sober - memory of when he had pinned me to the floor and asked me the same question. Did I know why he was in prison? It hadn't made sense at the time, I don't suppose it made sense to the poor victim either, but I was now very aware of how close I had become to being brutally raped.

It had a phone number at the bottom of the TV screen. It said, 'If any other woman had information pertaining to Steeple, don't be afraid to call.'

I immediately dialled the number. I said he had attacked me but that the police had intervened before he had a chance to do the harm that he had inflicted on his victim. I also said that I hadn't pressed charges because I wasn't aware of his history or what he was about to do to me.

The police couldn't understand why he was now living in Middlesbrough. I informed them that I guessed his secret had got out in Newcastle and he had fled for his welfare. Of course, I couldn't tell them he had literally been run out of town.

The poor Middlesbrough woman had been traumatised while I'd had a close escape. The fact that Crazy Karen had fought for her life and the police had turned up when they did, meant I hadn't suffered the same fate.

I reflected and again it dawned on me that I had been lucky, not unlucky. Perhaps my God had been looking out for me the whole time. I threw myself into recovery, hungry to learn.

I had also become really close to the midwife who had helped me through my pregnancy with Erin. She knew of my history because it came up as a red flag when she first took on my case. She asked if I'd be happy to tell others about my experience of growing up around alcohol and the impact it had on me, both as a child and an adult.

I wanted to give back to society and the institutions that had always been there for me when no one else was. I was beginning to realise that I was incredibly fortunate and would help in any way I could.

A huge conference was set up by Wansbeck Hospital in Northumberland and many professionals shared their theories, statistics and science-based facts about what was ruining children's lives and impacting on communities across the region. I sat there terrified, thinking, oh my God, these people really know what they're talking about and are using big, fancy words.

Fuck...I'm still living in a mad council estate, recovering from domestic violence and alcohol abuse. What the hell can I offer these educated people?

Again, I spent most of the morning in the toilets with a very loose bowel, and a hell of a lot of prayers were said before I took to the stage.

My legs felt weak, I was shaking, and my mouth was dry. The audience was made up of high-status people; doctors, social workers, professors, researchers and people who worked alongside the drug and alcohol services. They terrified me. How could I speak on a level playing field with that sort of audience?

I was trembling. I started to speak. Suddenly I couldn't stop, the words were just tumbling out. God was doing for me what I couldn't do for myself. He was using my experiences to get a message across.

I had no education, other than an HEFC in psychology that I still have no idea how I got, as I was pissed most of the time. But what I did have was experience. I'd had a life experience of drinking since the age of five, of growing up watching all the adults around me using it to numb their feelings. I had experience of domestic abuse and had relied heavily on addiction myself, especially through the abuse. I had experience of how it had impacted on my own family and the denial and madness that went with it. I talked about how I would lie to social services, terrified of the consequences and how even when I was pregnant, I couldn't abstain even though I wanted to so badly. I didn't hold back. It wasn't a time to hide; it was time to be honest. That was all I could give...honesty.

As I spoke, I realised I could help break the taboo and I could help these professionals understand why a mother lies to her children and peers, why an abused woman will stay, terrified of the repercussions, her esteem on the floor, feeling no one will believe her. Why she will hide and isolate and why she self-harms, either by physical means or psychological.

I could help, I could be of service, I really could, and it gave me inner strength.

I stood up to face the audience and spoke about becoming addicted to anything that changed how I felt, whether that be alcohol, men, exercise or food. How I had lived with shame and lies my entire life. How nobody even thinks about the addiction to prescription drugs and over the counter medication, like pain killers, cough medicine, anything to make you sleep, keep you awake or just take the edge off the nervous tension from a really long day. How woman and men like me will use and abuse anything they can get their hands on, rather than facing reality. How I desperately wanted help but was terrified of losing my children and how we come across as defensive as we hide our fear. How we judge ourselves harshly on a daily basis and if people just even tried to understand, we would open and pour our very souls out desperate for help. We weren't monsters; we were terrified, unwell people. We wanted to be just like the rest of society, instead of hiding. Frauds, masking our inadequacy. Oh my God, I had poured out my heart.

I ended my talk and the whole room stood up and applauded loudly. The tears welled up in my eyes. Oh my God! What was happening? And yet, it hit me straight away what was happening. In that moment I knew I could become a useful person not afraid to tell my truth. I was not a useless cunt.

I was elated. I was proud, it was unbelievable. Something in me had changed. I had found my calling.

23

My Daughter's Surprise

Me and Tommy stayed friends for a time, although his pride was hurt more than his heart. He quickly enjoyed his money and freedom and took our daughter on several lavish holidays and kitted her out in designer clothes costing thousands upon thousands of pounds.

I filed for divorce. I didn't take him to the cleaners like he presumed; I signed all the relevant papers to not pry into his businesses and accounts. The way I looked at it was that he had saved me, showed me another way to live. The last thing I wanted to do was to bankrupt the man and make money that I had never earned in the first place.

I left the marriage with nothing but my pride and freedom, but it was worth it. But Tommy being Tommy, became a victim. He made out I had fled with another man and that he funded my lifestyle. The truth was, I was skint and working voluntary, and was very content being single.

As time went by, he became more vengeful; he turned up at my house and gave me £50.00 maintenance. I don't know why, but I assumed he would look after us all. I had three children, one dressed in Chanel and the rest of us in Matalan.

Naively, I probably thought he would look after us financially because I left the marriage with no demands. He didn't, he thrived on showing me what I could have had, had I stayed with him. Once he realised his money was safe the anger and bitterness emerged. No amount of money was worth the control. I would rather be poor than be under his regime.

He still didn't want me to be free though and told anyone who would listen that I was his wife for the next fifteen years, whether I was there or not. After what I had lived through it seemed trivial. Tiring all the same.

One day at a time had rolled into weeks which rolled into months and then years and sobriety and life was stable and fulfilling. Devon was now eighteen years old and had been unsettled, saying that she felt a part of her was missing. She had reached the age where she could make decisions and had now wanted to find her father, but she had a lot of anxiety about it and about sharing that with me.

She hadn't wanted to hurt me and stir up old history.

We talked about the implications and how it could be difficult, and whether she had a realistic view about the whole concept. He could reject her, or he may be dead or in prison or even have a family of his own. Could she handle the great unknown, whatever that might be?

She thought long and hard and apparently had done so over the last couple of years.

Okay, I reasoned, then I would help her.

Over the years I sometimes had allowed myself to think about what had happened to Bob. I had never told Devon the extent of the reasons we never saw him again, but she knew I had lived in fear. However, if I thought it would give my daughter a sense of belonging, then I had a duty to support and care for her throughout the process. Over the years we had put his name into the computer from time to time, but to no avail. This time we used our own detective.

Within days he called back with an address and phone number for Bob's solicitor. Now all Devon had to do was forward a message. She was terrified and sat with the address for another couple of days and then she couldn't stop crying, not knowing what she would find.

I talked to her, 'Look, you will never know until you at least try. It's better to try and fail, than to have never tried, not knowing what might have been.'

We are all here to support you, I told her, and no matter what, we love you and want to help you.

To be honest, I was terrified he wouldn't want to know her. I was in a bigger mess than she was, but I had to act all calm and composed. Sara and Erin were cuddling their big sister, giving her moral support.

'Devon just dial the number,' I said.

She hummed and hawed, then bottled it and asked me to ring. I then hummed and hawed, then bottled it and asked Jan to ring.

Jan dialled the solicitor's number and passed on the message that Bob's daughter would like to get in touch. She left my home phone number.

The solicitor, over the next couple of days, had written a letter to Bob and while Bob was at work on the building site, his wife had received it and rang Bob. Bob, assuming it was something to do with his mother's will, asked his wife to open the letter while he was still on the phone. She read the message out to Bob that his long-lost daughter would like to make contact if he so wanted.

Apparently, his legs buckled, and he went weak and had to take a break. When he resumed his composure, he became incredibly excited to see the daughter he had not seen since that fateful night back in 1991, eighteen years ago. He immediately rang his solicitor and asked for the contact number.

The days that followed seemed surreal. We weren't sure if he had received his letter yet or if he even wanted to have contact with Devon. She was incredibly nervous and snapping at us all. God only knows what she was thinking.

It was a Tuesday night around 6.30pm when the phone rang. My heart stopped.

'Hello,' I said, waiting for a response.

In the strongest Cockney voice came a reply, 'Awight, is it possible to speak to Devon please?'

'Yes, yes, yes. I will get her for you...er...hang on.'

My heart started beating fast as I called on Devon to come to the phone. We hadn't expected a response, never mind this soon. It was both nerve-racking and exciting but could change at any point. Tense, I started to shake.

What if he tells her that he doesn't want any contact? What if he is angry that we've divulged a secret that he has kept all these years? What if he wants to hurt us? Oh God, my nerves.

Just then Devon came to the phone and she knew the call was important as it had affected my entire demeanour.

She took the receiver from my hand. I could see that she was absolutely terrified. The words wouldn't come out, she just sobbed her eighteen lost years into the phone.

I had never realised how much she had dreamt and hoped for this phone call. The tears fell down my face for my daughter. I was happy, she was happy, we were all happy.

They established a relationship via phone very quickly. They were constantly ringing each other. They would hang up, then ring each other back saying they wanted to talk more. It was beautiful to watch.

He asked if he could visit in the next few days. They had never known each other and had eighteen years of lost time to make up for. It was exciting, but secretly I was anxious. I didn't know what to expect or how to feel upon seeing him. My own feelings were all over the place, but this wasn't about me, it was about my first-born and I had to keep it together for her sake.

Within days Bob was back up in Newcastle and watching him run to his daughter to embrace was breath-taking.

He was nervous, it was plain to see, he probably wasn't sure of the reception he would get. His eyes caught mine and a softness fell over them. We attempted a casual hug that was both strange and somewhat awkward, but also pleasant, mature and respectful. I welcomed him into my house to have a quick cuppa and reacquaint.

They had so many similarities it was uncanny, they laughed at the same time at the same things and even had all the same mannerisms. Their noses and eyes were identical. They both couldn't believe what they were seeing and seemed elated to be in each other's company getting to know one another. My fears were tamed, and I had to face facts: it really was the happy-ever-after reconciliation. This was the best outcome a daughter and father could have.

As they went out to spend the day together, I went to buy a photo album and put together some photos of Devon during her childhood. When Bob came to say goodbye, I handed him the little gift. I had looked into his eyes only earlier that morning and now I looked into them again and saw sadness. Sadness and regret that he had missed his daughter growing up.

As me and Devon exchanged stories of her youth, his face told a story of loss. We couldn't undo those years, but I could share photos for him to keep.

'Here, this is for you. I know you've missed out on these years, but I hope this helps,' I said as I handed it over.

He stood still, visibly moved. In the album I had placed a card.

Thank you for coming up and making our daughter so happy. She had been lost and now she is found. I hold no grudges about the past and hope it is as healing for you as it is for me.

Wishing you all the very best.

Karen

Bob had never had any other children; he knew he had done wrong. He hadn't wanted to inflict what he had done to us on anyone else. His life had also spiralled out of control after that night in 1991. He had discovered heroin and it took some time before he had gone into rehab, cleaned up his life and settled down with a wife. For me, it put the monster in my dreams to bed once and for all.

24

Releasing the Last Demons

I spent fifteen years making amends to my children and society in general. Every motivational talk I did, I did free of charge. I did interviews for various newspapers as well as TV and radio work. I kept it anonymous for the sake of my children.

Since the conference for my midwife and the North East professionals had gone so well, we were inundated to carry the same message all over the region.

It snowballed.

We became a formidable force. There were two senior specialised midwives on board, trained in drug and alcohol; Dr Shonaz McKenzie, Senior Consultant of Wansbeck Hospital, and Helen Howlet, a top researcher. There was Marie Catterick, the founder of

FASD UK and author of *Understanding Foetal Alcohol Spectrum*, and myself, an ex-service user/speaker with real experience.

It was the perfect catalyst, it worked a treat, the professionals talking their hospital jargon with statistics, diagrams and knowledge, and me bringing it all to life. It had a massive impact and we took the message into every hospital and training facility that wanted to hear what we had to say.

It was brand-new at the time. Canada had known this stuff for years. America wasn't far behind but the UK, and the billions of revenue the alcohol industry made, took a lot of work to make people start to sit up and listen.

What quickly became apparent to me was that alcohol was toxic to a baby's brain in the womb, far more dangerous than a mother taking heroin. And yet, our culture and the generation before us, had always thought it was relatively safe. I would sit on the stage watching these clever people describing the hidden harms and symptoms and think, my Sara does that, she acts like that, she has problems like that. The more conferences we did, the more I secretly wondered if my midwife Val had asked me because she knew something I didn't.

A sobering thought and one that would make me feel sick to the stomach. So, I would shrug it off, thinking back to the cord around her neck. A lack of oxygen for God knows how long. There were definitely more problems than just ADHD, however this label sat more comfortably with me.

Radio stations were queuing up, they wanted more interviews, and the newspapers were now highlighting all the hidden harms of alcohol. We were making a difference in England and it was an amazing achievement.

We were delivering workshops and conferences on average once every six to eight weeks, and we all brought something different to the table. My experiences with alcohol, and the chaos that went with it, gave the professionals a platform to ask questions that the general public was uncomfortable to answer. My honesty and humility turned out to be my greatest assets.

Honesty helped me claim back some power. Power that I had so freely given away to others. I was always scared of someone saying, *I know about her, have you heard about her?*

I thought no one could use it against me if I disclosed my own demons and used it positively. Besides, it reads on the twenty-four-hour chip that you get after you're twenty-four hours clean from alcohol or drugs: *To thine own self be true.*

At first, I used to read that and wonder what exactly it meant. Then I realised. All my life I had wanted to be someone else. I yearned to be accepted. I just had to be true to myself first, then I could be true to others. I was sick of living in shame, now I wanted to be real. What I realised was that if someone has the courage to speak the truth about their lives, other people will follow.

I had always people-watched, mostly to stay safe or alive, now I was noticing what could make a difference.

I became held in high regard when it came to my recovery and my message. I went into women's refuges, probation meetings, hospitals, it was never-ending, and I relished it all.

I also learnt how to live on my own without needing to be rescued by anyone. I accomplished accreditation by going back to college to do various courses such as counselling, mentoring as life coach, neuro-linguistic practitioner and various holistic therapies for wellness. The joy I felt in helping women, women who were like me, was extremely rewarding. They were the ones that hid, and that society had given up on. I set up support meetings for mothers in recovery with children, and a meeting for adult children of dysfunction and addictions. I felt like I was fulfilling my purpose in life. I worked tirelessly, day and night. All voluntary...paying back my debt to the planet.

One morning I received a letter from The Public Health of England thanking me personally for my work. Life was incredible.

Occasionally I would bump into someone from my shady past and after the initial fear of impending judgment, I would hold my head high as I realised that I had changed and the ones still judging, hadn't. The men who thought I was worth nothing, were more troubled than me. If they had to get a woman drunk in order to get laid, then they were worse than me. And let's tell it how it is, a lot of men take complete advantage of women when drunk, and *No* really does mean *No*, drunk or sober.

Double standards, abuse, date rape, taking advantage of vulnerability. Yep, your card is marked now and we woman are becoming empowered.

My parents were blissfully unaware of my achievements, or if they were, they never once acknowledged it. Mam's friend once had asked me how I was and what I was up to. We got into a conversation about highlighting alcohol problems and the hidden harms. Mam quickly intervened and informed the friend I was unemployed although I had been a hairdresser. I just shrugged my shoulders and off I went.

Devon left the family home and moved down to Brighton to study music at the Brighton University. That was tough. Her dad, Bob, had bought a flat and was going to allow her to live there while studying. They had become inseparable and it was lovely to watch her grow and mature into a hardworking, focused young woman.

I moved to a beautiful rented house just outside Newcastle and left the council estate and the burden that went with it. It was a past I was happy to forget about.

Unfortunately, I didn't know that I would have to make a few more mistakes before I would be able to finally turn my back on dysfunction.

I could still lose myself to people's comments; I was still a people pleaser. If someone didn't like what I had said I'd worry about it weeks. It made me terrified of being assertive or of having a different opinion to that of other people. I was fearful of asking for my needs to be met, always conforming. I needed to become a shepherd, not part of the flock. I was also still full of self-doubt and would constantly have any newly found confidence shattered by someone's different view or cutting remark. I was becoming better, but just not as quick as I would have liked.

Tommy was still driving me mad by stalking the life out of me. He would drive by my new house and ring constantly, several times a day. On occasion he would let himself in and used the excuse it was for items and clothes needed for Erin. Such urgency, he simply couldn't wait. I knew what he was doing, he was checking in on me.

Any man who even came close to me was swiftly warned away.

It was driving me insane. I don't suppose I recognised the coercive control. After the abuse by the men in my past, this seemed mild in comparison. However, what I would come to realise in time was that it was still abuse. More subtle but debilitating all the same. He hid it well, disguised it as concern, monitoring my movements in case I needed his help. He reduced my maintenance in order to restrict my funds and undermined my abilities as both a woman and a mum. As usual he never listened to a word I had to say, he said I was being paranoid and over sensitive, and he had always tried to help. I tried to dismiss it and throw myself into work but, although I had been divorced for some time, I still felt trapped.

He threw lavish birthday parties for our daughter but did not invite me or her siblings. He painted a picture of me that I was disinterested in my child and he was the unsung hero saving the day.

My children were turning into young women. Sara was now a teenager, but she was haunted by her own demons and bad memories of the dysfunction I had bestowed upon her. She was attending college but kept getting into trouble. Like the last years of high school when she was suspended or threatened with expulsion.

She never learned from consequences and repeated the same mistakes. She had no concept of time or reasoning and was getting left behind by her peers. I would talk on the quiet to Maria Catterick, and Sara's behaviours were similar to the families we would talk about in the conferences. It weighed me down with guilt, so I just tried harder to pacify her.

Dean, Sara's dad, showed up after several years' absence and spoke to her about rekindling their fractured relationship. It wasn't fractured, it had been void, but I thought it would be good if they could salvage something.

I also hoped and believed that it would unfold like Devon's relationship with Bob and put the lid back on her self-destruction. Sara desperately wanted to have a relationship with Dean, more so as she had watched Devon and Bob's blossom into a loving father and daughter relationship. She secretly envied what they had and was desperate for the same.

Unfortunately, after a couple of reconciliations, Dean's wife, once again, became insecure and threatened causing all kinds of problems. She blamed Sara for being a bad influence on their children, and even drunkenly accused her of being sexually inappropriate. It made no sense. Sara was devastated at the extent this woman would go to ruin any sort of relationship she could rekindle with her dad. Defeated and broken, she started to despise her father for such weakness and broke all contact, never again to be mended. She hit that self-destruct mode even more and refused to see any of them ever again.

25

Confrontation

The calm before the storm came and once again me and my mam had a disagreement. As usual it was about the differences between my children and my sister's children. Please someone change the fucking record...

I had been mentioning the latest, crazy drink-fuelled incident relating to Sara, and my mam immediately told me that my children were like that because of me and how I had raised them. She went on to say what a disappointment we all were to her.

Like, seriously tell me something I don't know, would you? I thought to myself.

I listened, blah blah blah...failures, drunks, fucked up, let-downs.

Of course, they were not like my sister's children; I had been an addicted, drunken excuse for a punch bag. If anything, they should have been awarded medals for what they had put up with. I had been making amends every day I was sober, trying my hardest to remould my children's lives. I told Mam how Devon had enrolled into university, didn't that count for something? It was as if she hadn't heard me. She went off into a tirade of my faults and how I was nothing like my sister and her family.

My mother's fucking mantra.

As she was screaming insults at me, I recognised my thinking had started to shut down and I became silent and my body was now responding to the insults. I became stiff with anxiety, tense, I had an instant headache, my stomach knotted with fear and I felt nauseous. I couldn't talk and this was the first time I had recognised such a physical and mental reaction. The more shame I felt, the angrier I became and the less rational I was. I couldn't articulate my emotions, but my physiology kept the score. She clearly watched my body language and screamed at me, asking if I wanted her to leave. 'Well, do you? Do you want me to leave?' she balked.

In the past I would have talked myself out of this and pacified my mother whether she was right or wrong, frozen in fear. This time, still terrified but with enough strength to answer her, I said, 'Just go Mam, please.'

'Really, you want me to go?' Mam answered, hands on hip.

'Yes really, just go, please.'

It was progress, small, but in the right direction. I now had to reflect to process what had just happened.

Her harsh statements had produced intense feelings in my body. My thinking could never catch up quick enough, hence I would become numb. Sometimes it would take days or even weeks, depending on the circumstances, to make sense of such incidents. During this process I would be unable to function, I became easily distracted with outbursts of misdirected anger and I mentally closed down. It was confusing. It had always been confusing. I now know the term is referred to as 'disassociation'. Basically, it's a break in how my mind handles information. I become disconnected from my thoughts, feelings, memories and surroundings and it affects my identity and perception.

In a nutshell, my brain is warning me of impending danger and disappears to somewhere more pleasant, whilst my body gets ready for danger. I will either freeze, flee, or fight. A clever way of being in two places at the same time. God knows where I'd go, but somewhere less harmful. My body may then face the assault, but my mind would be elsewhere.

The disassociation could last for days, it was almost like a vacation and I would only come back when I felt safe. Then, and only then, could I perhaps articulate what had caused my upset. In the past this was when I'd either bury my head in the sand or brush what's left under the carpet. Never to make sense yet frustrated and incensed but not knowing why. My trigger was being shamed, humiliated or just good old-fashioned fear.

In this particular scenario with my mother, I recognised that it was both fear and the continued negative verbal shaming. I owed it to myself to confront it.

I found the courage to go to my mam's a week later. I was terrified and felt like a naughty child. I had written a letter as I thought it would help. I had only recently found my voice through attending support groups. It took forty-two years to be able to name and confront the feelings surrounding my relationship with my mother.

I was scared but hopeful and optimistic. It went down like a fucking lead balloon as I stood at her front door.

She had opened the door and stood on the step with her arms folded, immediately in the defensive.

I took a deep breath. 'Mam, why do you continuously put me and my kids down, why do you treat us differently to my sister and her family? Why do you shame us constantly, why do you never include us?'

Her face contorted and she answered, 'I don't.'

'Of course you do Mam, you go on holidays and you spend

Christmas together, you even have a caravan that my children have never been to. Your grandsons sleep over every weekend and have done so since they were born, my children have never slept at your house, they have never been invited. Why Mam, why do you treat my kids so differently?

Her face twisted in anger, 'I don't.'

I continued, 'You do Mam, you don't know my youngest, you've never wanted to. How can you deny the differences in the way you treat us? My family isn't perfect, I'm the first to acknowledge we have our problems, but I would have thought you'd be even more supportive because of that.'

And then her reaction.

'Karen, fuck off from my door,' she snarled.

'Mam, I knew you wouldn't listen to me.' I handed her the letter. 'Here, I've written a letter for you.'

'Karen, fuck off from my door and shove your fucking letter right up your arse.'

I climbed into my car shaking and crying, and the rage that filled my entire being felt like it would kill me there and then. Then it turned into rejection once again and the feeling of inadequacy quickly turned into self-loathing. The old familiar feelings of self-disgust and confusion were back.

My inner wounded child had been triggered to such an extent that I wanted to drive my car into the metro train at the back of Mam's house.

I couldn't use and I couldn't drink so I had to sit with the feelings of being worthless. Again.

I had to drive home to stay alive, scolding myself for confronting her. And yet I had asked a valid question. I knew the evidence was there to prove that what I had asked had was relevant. But here I was contemplating suicide and feeling worthless because of someone else's beliefs and actions and my distorted beliefs of myself.

I had clearly internalised the pain of rejection my entire life to the extent that I did it automatically. Children can't comprehend the fact that their abusers are abusers, especially if they are parents or carers, so they internalise the pain and make it their own. I was in my forties and still doing exactly this. I had to learn, I had to separate my feelings from what was real and what was just a result of the damage I had suffered over the years. However, I was recovering and in doing so I was finding my voice and becoming less confused by other people's actions. Rejection still hurt like hell though.

A few months later I was going into the shopping centre and saw my mother walking towards me. I didn't want to face her; it was an awkward moment, so I crossed the road. It was all about self-preservation now.

At midnight I got a text from my mam. *You're not so fucking brave without your vodka, now are you?*

This infuriated me, once again she was trying to shame me, calling me a coward.

I replied. *I crossed the road because I'm actually scared of myself and what I may have done to you.*

The hypocrisy, she was clearly drunk. But, true to form she turned the situation around and claimed to be the victim as she told everyone who would listen that I had threatened her by text.

26

Time for Healing

I was no longer a drunk and saw things a lot more clearly. My body still reacted in fear, but I was finding the strength to stand up to the person that I feared the most.

Anger had always been a motivator for me and when I picked myself up many weeks later, I set up a support group and I named it ACCEPT. It was an acronym for Adult Children Changing Emotional Problems Together.

If I hadn't had an outlet for my pain and confusion, I don't think I would be here today. Within the group we used some literature from the 12-step meetings of ACOA (Adult Children of Alcoholics) but tailored it to our own needs.

I studied the impact of dysfunction on children who grew up to be broken adult children, all nursing similar wounds. I learned that I wasn't born weak, but I reacted like a child when wounded. My body may have been in my forties but if shamed, scared or criticised I would react like a wounded infant. The numbness that followed such incidences was me dissociating. It was a coping mechanism established as a helpless child living through repeated trauma for a lengthy time. It explained the memory lapses and confusion that followed anything that produced fear. I was beginning to see everything clearly while patiently analysing every action and reaction.

The ACCEPT members all had similar coping mechanisms. These had served us well as children but hindered us as adults. We all had immense fear of authority figures, usually our parents or abusers. We had lost our identities, confused about who we were. We were terrified of angry people and any personal criticism. Our lives were ravaged by addictions or ruled by rescuing sick people. We were co-dependent. We had immense guilt when standing up for ourselves. We scorned ourselves harshly and were terrified of abandonment; trapped in our inner child, tormented and frozen in childhood. The list went on and on.

The solution was to recognise these traits in a safe environment and unravel the coping mechanisms that were no longer helpful. Our experiences taught us that until we knew how to set boundaries to stay safe, it was best to give conflict and toxic people a wide berth. That meant avoiding my own mother.

I had to learn to nurture myself. I hadn't self-soothed; I had always looked for a man to do that for me. Living in fear meant my body became addicted to the adrenalin that fear produced and as a result I constantly looked for something to worry over so I could receive my regular high.

I lived in the meetings by attending regular AA, ACOA and ACCEPT sessions for the next few years and identifying with like-minded people; all lost, trapped in our broken childhoods and reacting in unhealthy ways.

Addiction was my solution for the hate that was projected onto me. Self-disgust was my symptom. I wasn't just an alcoholic, I was also an adult child, re-enacting my family's blueprint of madness and blame. I was both alcoholic and an adult child.

Until I addressed this, I would always resort to my own dysfunctions. I would always choose a partner that represented my dad. I would always look for traits of my mother's callous words or actions in both friends and work colleagues. History would play like a broken record over and over unless I healed from the inside out.

Much easier said than done, as my body and mind will always seek out the familiar, and the norm for me was pain of an emotional, physical or sexual nature. Self-hate was my core, I felt unlovable and unworthy based on my parents and my partners' beliefs. I had to change my internal dialogue.

I used hypnotherapy, self-help books and support meetings. This had been the hardest thing to overcome and I would put in a lot of time and effort into rebuilding my worth, only to have it dismantled by another person's words or actions.

My parents had their faults as I had mine, but they still painted a lie while the world watched mine. My childhood was dismissed, and I was told it was not as it seemed. My self-doubt believed that for a while, but the reality was very different. What I resist will unfortunately persist. I had to break the chain of pain and tell it how it was.

It was painful, not for a little time, but for most of the time. I couldn't get on a stage and be honest about my failings if I still kept secrets about my parents' failings.

For the next several years I studied everything that I could and kept my distance from Mam and Dad until I could maintain boundaries. I felt guilt for standing up to Mam and walking away but it was necessary. My wellbeing had to come first. I prayed daily for the wisdom to know if, and when, I may need to rekindle my relationship with my mother. For now, I was concentrating on my own children and the people from the support groups.

I had been working with a child psychologist as part of the FASD movement and asked him if I could email him a list of behaviours that Sara was constantly displaying. He said he could do one better and would forward us an evaluation form. It would be basic, without a full assessment but would give us an idea of some of the recurring issues we were having. If I needed any further assistance, he said to not hesitate to get in touch.

Sara was unable to hold down jobs. Her behaviour constantly got her fired. She was also losing friends regularly and abusing alcohol persistently. Her new acquaintances were incredibly dangerous and unpredictable. I was running around in circles trying to clean up her mess and keep her safe. Her life was increasingly chaotic. It was becoming so unpredictable that I began to fear for her life.

I filled out the form and sent it back to the psychologist and he was eager to come and help. Sara, however, was having none of it. She hated the labels thrown at her, she hated everything that labelled her differently than her peers. I was relieved when she turned up one day with a boyfriend that she wanted to settle down with. Perhaps now she would be okay? The evaluation form, with its contents, was safely filed away in that internal cabinet of mine.

I had heard from family members that my mother was poorly, and I know I was judged for not arriving sooner, but it had to be when I was strong enough. I had continuously prayed for the wisdom to know the right time to visit.

The sun was shining through my bedroom window when I woke one day, and I knew that today was the day to see both my parents. I can't explain how I knew but it was an overwhelming feeling of 'This is the day and it's going to be okay.'

I got dressed and said to Sara, 'Okay, today I'm visiting my mam and dad.'

Her mouth fell open and stayed that way for what seemed like forever. It had been years since I'd saw my parents. I wasn't sure what to expect but I knew I had changed. However, I was afraid that all my hard work might unravel if my parents continued to reject or abuse me. I said prayers all the way to their house, for strength, courage and tolerance.

I knocked at their window and waved. Dad looked too frail to be answering the door, so I took a deep breath and walked in. My mother was looking old and seemed unable to move from her chair. We collectively burst into tears. Not gentle tears, but heartfelt ones; we cried at our years of loss. It was genuine sorrow, a natural release of pain and disappointment running down all our faces. No words were needed, just hugs and warmth and hope.

We never mentioned our past difficulties and disagreements. We didn't have too. All that mattered was now. I was taken aback in shock, especially at how old and fragile my mother had become. She had been diagnosed with Parkinson's PSP disease (Progressive Supranuclear Palsy). Because the disease progresses at such a rate, Mam could no longer walk. She had deteriorated at quite some speed and was now cared for by my dad.

It was sad to see that this once feisty woman had hung up her boxing gloves and was now a frail old woman. She posed no threat at all. She seemed to accept her diagnosis too, which I didn't expect. It sounds awful to admit, but I had wondered how poorly she really was at first, as she hadn't had a good track record for telling the truth about her condition. Yet here she was, clearly broken and frail. It was plain to see the illness had taken a hold of her. I felt sad.

She gave a slight grin. 'I knew you would come; I've had a feeling all week.' She now smiled softly.

This took me by surprise, although I knew it was the right time to visit. I had trusted in divine intervention and it seemed incredibly timely. I returned the smile. We never did have too much to say, we never would. Our awkwardness around each other would remain and yet we both sensed time was running out. We knew that this was the time to put our differences and battles aside.

Mam was looking out into the garden in deep thought and I instinctively knew what she was thinking.

I looked at her and whispered, 'Mam, God is not punishing you, you know.'

'Is He not, how do you know?' she said still staring at the shrubs.

'Because even innocent children get horrible illnesses.' I said gently.

That was as close as it got to us ever figuring it all out. What was the point of trying to analyse our history? What was done was done, and with the short time we had left we would build bridges. Rickety bridges but bridges all the same.

27

Good night

As Mam's Parkinson's got progressively worse, Dad started suffering with ill health too and

Mam was admitted into a care home to be looked after around the clock. I again intuitively knew that my dad would go downhill quickly. I knew he was the most vulnerable. I wanted to help him as much as I could. It was difficult seeing him old, fragile and full of fear. My dad, the angry, hateful man, was now terrified.

The family were visiting Mam most days and tending to her needs and I sneaked right on in there to help Dad. I would never have been allowed to have a relationship otherwise.

On hearing he was refusing to get out of bed since Mam went into the home I went and knocked on his door. At first, he refused to answer it. I knocked louder. I looked through the window and he called out to him.

'No, go away, I don't want company. Go on, piss off.'

I took a deep breath and replied, 'If you don't fucking answer this door immediately, I'm coming in through the window.'

To my amazement he jumped up in a panic saying, 'Okay pet.'

It was as easy as that. I sat him down and took another deep breath and in a matter of fact way, told it how it was. 'Dad I know you don't like company, and don't even like us kids, but you need us, you need your family and we are the only ones left to help you. Whether you like it or not, we are all you've got, and we are here to stay.'

He stayed quiet.

'You're not well and you're frail, tired and scared. Let me help you.'

I have no idea where the courage had come from. This was the man who had terrified me most of my life, but it was sad seeing him so scared.

He nodded his head and eventually said, 'Okay.'

It was the start of a fabulous healing time for both of us. I started to do his washing and we would go shopping. We became friends for the first time in our lives. I was forty-nine years old.

I stopped all the voluntary work and concentrated on being there for my dad and visiting Mam in-between. I knew it would be a short time. My dad became my best friend and I got him various vitamins and pushed him to leave his house. Eventually he started to accept the circumstances and became less depressed and more motivated to get physically well. Mad really. My parents had fought tooth and nail throughout their marriage, yet he missed Mam terribly when she went into the home. He kept saying that she had left him. We had to reassure him she didn't have a choice; they were both too unwell to carry that burden.

It wasn't easy, we all became our parents' carers. We all had families but were there every step of the way.

As structure formed, and everything settled somewhat, I picked up some part-time work from home as I needed the money. I had just had an interview for a couple more hours and it had gone well. The phone rang and I skipped over to pick it up. It was the police. Dad had been in a car accident. They told me not to worry, it was very superficial, but he had driven into a parked car and took a bump to the head.

By time I got to the hospital my sister was already there and our brother was on the way. Dad was sitting up in bed in A&E, but he was very confused. He knew who we were, but nothing else. The doctor wanted blood, which Dad detested. In the past he would become violent and try to punch the perpetrator for taking bloods. Over the last ten months me and Amy would restrain him when they needed samples. This day we couldn't, and he became incredibly distressed and agitated. We were ushered outside while they attempted to draw blood and calm our dad down. A minute or two later we heard a very strange noise, a banging on the bed and a strange, gurgling sound. Amy put her head around the curtain and screamed. Dad was having a seizure and was shaking violently on the bed.

My sister became hysterical, so I grabbed hold of her with force and took her away whilst doctors and nurses were rushing in and around the room. Just like the old days I comforted her; I didn't want her to watch that. I knew she would forever replay that image. I held her tightly as time stood still. Several minutes later the nurse advised us to sit in a side room and they rushed by, taking Dad off for a CT scan. I promised my sister that everything would be okay. It wasn't to be. The next time we saw our father he was on a life-support machine.

My dad spent the next four weeks in the ITU and his whole body stopped working, one organ after another closing down, like lights in a house at night going out one by one. He never regained consciousness and we watched him pass away as the machine was turned off on 19 October 2017.

I was devastated. I felt like I had just got acquainted with my dad, the dad he was always meant to be, and then he had been taken away from me. Seeing him so scared made all the bad memories fade. I had forgiven him and loved him dearly. Those ten months that we had together were priceless and I honestly believe they were meant to be just like that. They were perfect...as if everything had been healed.

Mam took a turn for the worse after Dad's death and was in and out of hospital with heart failure. Her organs were also starting to close down, and she kept coming down with infections. All her emotions had gone, as did all her faculties. It was incredibly difficult being in and out of the RVI, trying to make sense of my new reality.

Devon had just recently moved back home to Newcastle to spend time with her grandparents. She had completed her degree and left a successful job to be back with her family. She was twenty-six years old. Sara was now twenty-two and had eventually completed the psychologist's evaluation relating to her behaviour patterns. The psychologist had visited her to do a full evaluation and assessment of her cognitive abilities and within hours was giving a diagnosis of Foetal Alcohol Spectrum Disorder (FASD).

My dad's death became a catalyst for both my daughters and they simultaneously decided to hit the 'Fuck it button' and spiralled into their own addictions, which resulted into total madness and a rapid decline of their health, especially their mental health.

Sara lost the plot entirely and was extremely angry with her diagnosis along with her mother who had suggested it in the first place. She also couldn't handle the trauma of having watched her grandad pass away together with the remnants of her father's rejection. They were all too much to bear. Like a perfect storm she hit self-destruct and ended up abusing cocaine and alcohol to levels so high, I was terrified I was going to find her dead or murdered. It was my worst nightmare come true. She roared through everyone's life like a deadly hurricane, causing carnage and scattering debris left right and centre. It was sheer chaos as she destroyed everything in her way, leaving broken fragments of everyone's life behind.

Her denial of using meant she couldn't see the destruction she was creating and living in. Her chaotic lifestyle represented her chaotic thinking: erratic, unpredictable and unstable. It was horrendous to watch.

Dad's funeral approached; God knows how she would cope.

28

Madness

Dad had a wonderful send-off; his family had done him proud. I didn't want to stay at the wake as I was tired. Watching Sara and her boyfriend getting louder and louder and more unpredictable, I decided it was time to go. I left and dropped Devon off too, thankfully she didn't want to join in the drowning of sorrows either.

The next day was still and quiet and sombre. I was enjoying the quiet stillness, the calm before the storm. I had retired to bed early as I was still extremely tired and fell into a deep sleep. I woke up to Devon screaming and thought I was dreaming. It took a minute or two to realise it wasn't a dream but in fact Devon was screaming, right there in my bedroom. Nothing was making sense; she was screaming that Sara's boyfriend had attacked her and smashed up her car.

'Slow down Devon, I can't understand what you're saying,' I said jumping out of bed, all disorientated and dazed.

Hysterically she said, 'Billy has just beaten me up and smashed my car, Mam.'

'Er, why? Nothing is making sense, where?

'He turned up looking for Sara and bounced off all the walls, drunk and high. Look, look,' she said, holding out her hand, gripping half her long hair. Now she touched her head and hair was coming out by the handful.

Oh my God, this is not a dream, it's real. What the fuck is happening?

I was still dazed and couldn't think straight and wasn't sure what to do. The funeral had been the day before. Had Billy and Sara stayed high since then?

'Where is Sara? Where's Billy now?'

'I don't know. I left them to come here. I've rang the police!' Devon was screaming hysterically.

Nothing made sense. I was frantically trying to piece everything together.

Apparently, Billy and Sara had stayed high for forty-eight hours and became volatile with each other. Sara thought it best to leave Billy's house and take refuge at Devon's place. The problem was that Billy got there first. He was highly irritable and incoherent. Devon was sober and scared and asked him to leave, but this just fuelled his irritation. He became aggressive, smashed the front door and the car outside and then attacked Devon.

Sara turned up and didn't know what to do as she watched her boyfriend and sister fight.

She watched the mayhem unfold and fell to her knees.

Oh God, oh good fucking God, the whole family was falling apart, and I felt powerless to help them.

Anger followed soon after as the realisation of what had

happened, dawned on me. Drink and drugs were again to blame for destroying our family.

I was angry, I was grieving, and I couldn't deal with Sara's addiction and mayhem. I pushed forward with the paperwork and her diagnosis, to provide some wraparound care for her future. I tried to get her a social worker and some help to get her off the drink and drugs that she was using most days, but she wasn't ready. In fact, now her relationship with Billy had ended, she was even worse.

Christ, you couldn't make this up, I thought.

Nevertheless, I worked tirelessly in the background trying to get her into her own accommodation. It was beginning to affect my own sobriety. Alcohol was starting to look appealing again.

I had caused this illness of Sara's. I felt torn. It was my fault. Why should I be so healthy and sober when she was in this mess?

Mam was in and out of the RVI. It was an incredibly difficult time.

After the assault, Devon became clinically depressed and was on suicide watch. Both my children were now lost in addiction. I started having panic attacks, I was drained and constantly tired. I could see no light at the end of the tunnel. I was spinning so many plates that it was inevitable something would give, and I would drop the lot.

And, wouldn't you know, my vulnerability had attracted a man who said everything I needed to hear at that time. He said all the soothing, caring and supportive words that a woman like me so easily believes and craves to hear. He had heard of my father's death, he offered support, condolences and care. It wasn't real, it most definitely wasn't fucking real, but I wasn't thinking straight. It was a distraction for me to have light in the darkness that was now constantly hovering above my head. It was one of the biggest mistakes of my life and cost me everything at the time.

Mam was admitted into hospital for the very last time in April 2018. We were told her heart and organs were failing and she had only days left to live. We watched her sink into a comatose state, fuelled by the morphine given to make her more comfortable. She had her family around her, and we all kept vigil so that she wouldn't be alone when she passed. I played her songs of Devon singing and her favourite songs that Dad used to sing.

It broke my heart watching my sister say her goodbyes to her best friend. It was an image of heart-wrenching pain.

She died peacefully on Tuesday morning, 17 April. Within five months we had buried both our parents.

I had many a sleepless night worrying about everything, especially my children. I knew they were grieving but the drama that went with it filled me with anxiety. Sara was still living with me, but it was incredibly fractured. I was still cleaning up the wreckage of my past at fifty years old. My guilt around the whole diagnosis was an invisible chain running me into the ground trying to save her.

Conflicting thoughts mixed with grief is a confusing thing. I started to sink. The man I was dating, the man who I thought was going to look after me during this difficult time had been cheating with his ex, who quickly sold him out. I was bankrupt in all areas of my life.

I should have gone back to the AA. I had not been there for some time, which made me lack the healthy support that got me to being sober for just under fifteen years.

29

Rock bottom

An advert came on the TV and it was for the new pink gin. I caught myself playing with the fantasy and temporarily shook it off, but I knew what was coming. If I could just let loose for a little bit, I reasoned with myself. Everyone else is, why not me? My thinking had found all the justification it needed, and within hours I ended up in the local pub. I'll just have one, I thought to myself.

The glass was huge, the colour was pink with the ice sparkling like diamonds. It looked beautiful and my mouth instantly watered. I brought it to my lips. The cold gin warmed up my insides and the worry of the last seven months faded into the background. It was bliss. It was a hot sunny day and I wandered into the beer garden. I had found my way back into temporary heaven that quickly turns to permanent hell.

An alcoholic does not stop being alcoholic just because they haven't had a drink in a while.

The illness had still been progressing in the background as I found out by immediately going on a three-day drinking spree. I came to in my house, surrounded by three empty bottles of pink gin. I was ill with alcohol poisoning. I took to my bed, feeling like death, for days, promising myself that it would never happen again. I meant every single word.

A few months later Christmas Day was approaching, and I hadn't had a drink since the three-day bender over the summer. But I hadn't stopped thinking of it either. The chaos with Sara, the death of my parents and the partner who had betrayed me, had left me dangerously low in the wellness department. I was back wondering what the point was and thinking about how unfair life was. Recovery seemed a million miles away and I wondered how I had ever stood on stages giving talks when I was now so terrified to leave my house. I reached for a bottle of wine. At least it wasn't gin I thought. I enjoyed the calm, but I struggled to put it back down. It wasn't madness like my previous drinking career, but it would have turned into that for sure. Thank God I'd had multiple years of sobriety and something to measure this relapse with, as it reinforced the idea that life, for me, is better sober. However, at this point it was impossible for me to stop.

Within months I was even more of a nervous wreck, the alcohol was adding to my anxiety and depression and I couldn't think straight whatsoever. I couldn't function at all, I felt overwhelmed, couldn't concentrate or tackle problems, I couldn't even keep up with the basics like school emails, the phone or mail. Everything seemed to be falling on top of me.

I had to get my life back together and that meant recovery, but I had forgotten how.

The first thing I had to do was get rid of the waster I was dating, the man who was fleecing me and taking the piss. Him, and the carnage he brought with him, had to go. I prayed for the strength. God will do for me what I can't do for myself.

We were having a drink in the local pub and, believe it or not, he tried to steal a purse. That's all I needed to see. He was dropped off at Central Station and told never to return. As soon as he had gone, so did the carnage that followed him: the lies, the stealing, the baggage. The madness that had come with him.

Within weeks he was in prison for theft. The newspaper clippings and my personal details were kindly plastered all over my social media account by his ex. *Man who specialises in theft from vulnerable women is back behind bars after robbing an old woman of £10,000. He had a long history of manipulation and stealing from women.*

Wow, knock me down with a feather. Here we go again. What the hell is wrong with me to even allow these cunning people into my life? Why can't I see through them?

I wasn't so much angry with him as I was with myself. I spiralled further into a depression that lasted months. I couldn't, and wouldn't, leave the safety of my house. I fell back into watching fantasy and mystical, magical things on the TV, lost in an illusion because reality hurt.

And I was still battling with the alcohol, not that I was drinking copious amounts but when I did drink, I couldn't stop and the way it made me feel was awful. A head full of AA and a belly full of alcohol just does not mix. A gigantic failure. I had no purpose and I had failed myself, my family and the people I had once helped.

I was the epitome of a very unempowered woman.

I went back to AA but struggled to stay sober longer than two weeks. I felt like a fraud. There was a constant stream of new faces coming into recovery and they all seemed to be getting sober. Me, I couldn't stay abstinent. The more I struggled, the more I drank. I worried about never getting any clean time back.

I had watched people relapsing and disappearing over the years. Many never made it back, a lot died. At least I had half a chance by being back, even if it was crippling my pride. For seven months I wrestled with putting the cork back in the bottle.

It had been a beautiful day and it was a beautiful evening; the nights were orange and fresh. I settled down to watch some TV and the time was 8.45pm. I was fourteen days sober.

The insatiable desire to have a pink gin came from nowhere. There was no rhyme or reason, my disease of alcoholism had struck. I tried to rid the thoughts in my head that were now screaming, and it just wouldn't ease. For the alcoholic, it's like being possessed. The thought pops into your head and starts fighting with your brain, giving you any justification you want to reach for a bottle. The pull is like a magnet, every vein in your body is pulsating for a hit. The conflict is loud, but the winner is the disease and every excuse seem relevant at the time. It doesn't matter if you can afford it or not, you will find a way. It doesn't matter if the shops are closed, you will find a way and you acquire it and it doesn't give a toss what you'll lose in the process. Whether that is a partner, your children, your house, your job, it matters not.

The pull cannot be thwarted without a defence system in place. I hadn't fully surrendered to believe the fact that I couldn't control alcohol. That I never could control it and I never would.

The desire to drink was so overwhelming that it was impossible not to give in to temptation. No matter how many times my past proved that it all goes wrong when I drink, I will still go and drink. This is the disease part, like the devil is battling with all those good intentions and laughing at me when he succeeds again. If I do succumb to that first drink, well, all bets are off.

I had every intention to have just a couple of pink gins and go to bed. I know from experience that this has never happened, however I believed I could do it. I would have two gins and then go to bed. No harm in that, I reasoned.

That was the illusion. The reality was that I went into blackout early on and clearly my two gins rule went out the window.

Stepping through the doors into the world of an alcoholic and it's dreamlike and fun, but it soon becomes dark and lonely, filled with despair and doom. Thinking becomes distorted and illusions warped, and back to front, in a very short time. I had ten hours of nothingness to recall. No memory of what I done, what I watched and what I ate, if I did. All I can recall is coming out of blackout and being conscious of the time. It was 7am and I was devastated that I had crossed that invisible line again, which for me was drinking into the next day. The guilt, remorse and horror just fuelled my desire to go into another blackout as quick as possible, so that I didn't have to face my reality. I googled the shop opening times and headed straight to the corner store for another bottle of gin. Blinds closed and in my own world I started on the second bottle.

It was going to end badly, it was inevitable. My thinking would always slip further into misery and self-pity, it came like a side dish to the alcohol.

By now I was riddled in toxic shame, thinking that I can't clean any of this mess up and I certainly cannot live life on life's terms. I never could and I never would.

There was no logical way I could redeem myself. It doesn't take long from the pleasurable alcoholic feelings to become either homicidal or suicidal. In this incident, my thinking had returned to self-hate. Once I'm in this frame of thinking, nothing, and I mean *nothing*, can change it. It's scary how quickly thoughts take over and even scarier how easy it is to act impulsively in that state. The demon gives you the courage to carry out the madness of the insane thinking. There's no going back at this point.

So, I thought, fuck it. I wanted out of this mess. I was standing in the kitchen and took my shiny, new razor blade, from the barbering course I had completed earlier in the year and took it across my wrist. This time there was no room for failure. I took a deep breath and pressed hard into the skin and sliced straight across my flesh and only stopped pressing when the blade hit something hard. I was amazed at the resultant explosion of colour. I had successfully hit an artery and the blood spurted high in the air.

I wasn't scared, I was relieved. I would soon be out of this misery and my pain would finally be over once and for all. Finally. Mission accomplished.

God had other plans for me. My friend walked in on the scene. (She later told me she'd had a weird feeling that something wasn't right and because I wasn't answering the phone had decided to call round.) She went into autopilot and her training as a fire officer immediately took hold. She calmly laid me down on the floor and elevated my arm, wrapping it in two tea towels. She then removed her sweatshirt and wrapped that tightly around my arm, too. My poor friend will probably never get that image out of her head. No words can erase that, no number of apologies or flowers will take that picture away. I'm sorry…from the bottom of my heart.

The paramedics came and the last I remember was that they gave me morphine. Ironic really, as I felt no pain whatsoever. However, the addict in me was grateful to be induced with this pleasurable substance. Might as well die on a high, I thought, as the substance soothed my noisy head and bliss rushed through my veins. No wonder the addict stays hooked on heroin. That peaceful state where nothing matters and you're finally feeling good.

I was out of it for several hours. I was awake, but it's all foggy and I can't remember much. As late evening approached the euphoric medication had subsided and my reality was hurting again. Oh my God, what the fuck have I done?

My arm was heavily bandaged and still elevated, tied with a tourniquet. I was in a surgical ward in the RVI and felt guilty as my injuries were self-inflicted, and the poor women that resided with me were all having or had surgery through no fault of their own.

I couldn't talk, I just cried. I had hit my rock bottom on all accounts. Physically, mentally and spiritually I was broken. I was in the loneliest place on the planet, a place where you quietly beg for sleep, for some relief.

At first light I was taken down for surgery to be put back together. My spaghetti arm, and that's a term that I haven't made up, was all mangled, loose wires protruding and it was attached to some sort of electrical machinery.

It was difficult to know what went where. The artery was cut, and I had severed three tendons and all of the muscle belly. God only knows how these genius surgeons joined that all together again. They were waiting to get started and I received an anaesthetic block to my arm, like an epidural, so that I would remain awake for the repair of the mess I had made. As the surgeon unwrapped my arm to operate, on removing the tourniquet the blood spouted high into the air, only this time I was sober, and it was a shock to see. As the blood flowed, the heart monitor started to slow down dangerously, and I silently begged for sleep. My prayer was 'Dear God, please turn off that bloody machine.'

I've no luck, I thought, as that bloody machine picked up the pace and started to beep more rapidly. A tear rolled down my cheek and a young male nurse said, 'Are you alright? You shouldn't be feeling any pain.' He then he wiped the tears running noiselessly down my face.

I answered him softly, 'No I can't feel anything, it's my thoughts that are hurting.'

The surgery consisted of putting my tendons back together, repairing an artery and reconstructing the muscle belly wall. I was placed in an arm splint and taken back to the ward. My phone pinged and I checked it. It was from the school: my records were being removed. Tommy was now Erin's sole carer.

I had lost everything, and I couldn't do anything about it.

30

Hope

The next few hours were dark and still. I was paralysed with fear and regret. I was hopelessly powerless over the situation. I closed my eyes and said the Serenity Prayer.

God grant me the serenity to accept the things I cannot change, courage to change the things I can and the wisdom to know the difference.

There were no flashing lights or a mystical being appearing, but I have no explanation of how I went from feeling gripped by fear and despair to total acceptance. Acceptance of everything. A feeling of divine love washed over my body and I felt calm and safe and at peace. I have no idea how, or why, and I certainly did not feel worthy of it, but it happened, and I fully embraced it.

Nothing mattered.

I just had to breathe and trust. I instinctively knew that everything would eventually be all right. I had let go. Were my prayers being answered?

I had never let go of anything. It was a total relief. All I had to do was trust in something bigger than me running the show. Complete acceptance.

As usual, I saw the hospital Psychiatric Liaison team and calmly and honestly told them how I had regressed after the trouble surrounding my daughters, my ex and the deaths of my parents. I told them about the conflicting thoughts I had, the guilt I felt and my battle with alcohol.

I had basically had a breakdown. My psychiatric assessment was a positive read considering what I had just lived through. It was validation of how powerless I had been, faced with the circumstances that had surrounded me over the last year. The chaos had contributed to my meltdown and, in a way, had been inevitable. My record of dependency and self-harm was there in black and white. My history of dating unsavoury and manipulative men fulfilled a prophesied future of doom and abuse to play out.

I'd suffered a childhood of beatings and berating. I hadn't made any of it up. It was real, the evidence was there. When my parents had died the grief had stirred up conflicting feelings, confusing but begging to be processed. And though I had searched over the years for help to make sense of my past, I had never had treatment for post-traumatic stress disorder (PTSD). In fact, it was the first time I had had my circumstances validated.

I was deemed more than capable, as long as I stayed sober. I was to be heard and helped and offered therapy to address the PTSD. This acceptance lark was turning out to be more than helpful. It was a priceless life skill.

I had survived abuse at the hands of the very people I had trusted and loved the most, my parents and partners. It had left scars on my body and soul that changed how I viewed myself and my surroundings. I wasn't mad or weak, I had survived a bloody battle.

I was released from hospital several days later, plastered up to my elbow. I couldn't do anything but recuperate and read and practice self-care. The amazing thing about rock bottom is you cannot go any further down, only up.

I had lost everything, my children, the use of my arm, my self-respect and my job.

It was in losing myself that I found myself. A great paradox, but true. It would be the first time in my life I admitted to myself that I was totally powerless over my past. I couldn't do anything other than accept the situation. I knew I was powerless over alcohol and this was the second time I had admitted complete defeat against the drink. I had no desire whatsoever in even toying with the idea that alcohol was for me. But I had always tried hard to orchestrate my surroundings and be in some kind of control. This time I couldn't. I could literally only manage to comprehend living in the day and accepting what would be, no matter what that was.

While recuperating I read feverishly, and I read how the body keeps score of trauma and how I would have to put effort into changing how I viewed the world. How I had conditioned myself to fail, to be abused, to just exist. But because I had conditioned myself to do these things, I could choose another way. I also read spiritual books and hung tight to my faith, which had been magnified, not lessened. I even read the book of Job, with the hope that if I kept doing the right thing, the right things would happen for me.

I had to be accountable and own all my madness and bad choices. I had to, for once, take my head out of the sand to see. Only when I could forgive myself could I begin to forgive others. When I could understand the subconscious actions, only then could I see the reactions and consequences. Painful at times, but you just can't ignore them once you can see them all. I could see how my defence mechanism had tried to protect me, but sometimes hurt me more in the process, how my biggest enemy was never outside of myself but within me. And if I called an amnesty to self-hating behaviour, I could become friends with myself and my past, but especially with my future.

Sometimes we must die before we can live. The old me had died. The new me was being reborn. Like a phoenix emerging from the ashes, I was determined to be stronger and wiser, more powerful than before.

I was back in AA meetings, fragile, but determined, sharing where my last drink had taken me. Again, I was instructed to just own my truth no matter how reckless it made me sound, as I would be able to help another person. I couldn't possibly understand how, but I was assured that I could.

I guess the strongest message I could give was that my sobriety of almost fifteen years was not as safe as I had presumed. I told the recovery world that my reckless choices in men were so dangerous for people like me and trying to save my family from their own addictions were detrimental to my health. Instead, as AA suggests, 'I had to let go with love and whatever will be will be'.

Something told me there was a book in me and I began to write. I couldn't stop. It was like I had taken the lid off Pandora's Box and fifty-one years of my fucked up, broken and fragmented parts all came tumbling out. I couldn't type, only use a pen, and wrote frantically, unravelling my story, my life, my pain and mistakes. Putting it all down and in order quietened my head, which immediately benefited my body. I would go to meetings, read and write and only live in the day. It was manageable.

I picked up my 1-week sober chip from AA.

Tommy had taken my daughter and rightfully so, but his control and the lengths he would go to, to maintain that control were becoming insane and dangerous for our wellbeing. Again, he had let himself into my house and removed all our daughter's clothes and electrical devices. He never asked how I was, just that I wouldn't be receiving any more maintenance, and to this day I still haven't. He refused to give Erin back, even though social services had closed the case. I had nothing left in me to fight with. But for now she was safe, and I would concentrate on my own recovery. I would let him play his game.

I picked up my 1-month sober chip from AA.

Every time Erin was going to come visit me, Tommy distracted her with expensive designer clothes and Yeezy trainers or box office football trips. It hurt like hell, but she was now fourteen and I had put fourteen years into that relationship. She would be back.

It was the first time in my life I had no responsibilities and just had to think about taking care of me. It was daunting, yet strangely refreshing and calming. Ever since I could remember, I had always been someone's caretaker.

Sara was still chaotic and abusing drugs to suicidal proportions, but I had made peace with the fact that it wasn't my job to save someone who didn't want saving. It was a relief to have handed over the burden and now she was drinking and using with my sister. I knew that if the worst happened that I had done everything in my power to try and help her. She abused drugs right up to the day she overdosed, had a seizure and was hospitalised. She decided on her own that enough was enough. I prayed that she'd had her rock bottom also.

Within weeks of recovering and detoxing she put her name down for a boxing charity match and started training for fitness and discipline. She beat her opponent comfortably and it spurred her on to keep the boxing up. Her life today is a million miles away from the life she lived. Up to now she is undefeated, settled with a girlfriend and helping troubled young children to use fitness as a release, not alcohol and drugs. Who knew? I stopped rescuing her and she ended up rescuing herself. It was meant to be...just like that.

Devon settled with a boyfriend and also reigned in the alcohol use. She became a high achiever who is working incredibly hard to save the money so that one day she can reside abroad and have a brand-new start. Perhaps my spell in hospital shook both my kids up to the point they had no choice but to change their own lives.

Or perhaps they just wanted better.

What I do know is the day I stopped trying to fix them and concentrated on my own wellness was the turning point for them to do the same.

Devon visits her father regularly. They have an amazing bond.

I picked up my 6-month chip from AA.

Tommy took on more than he could chew. After getting praised for saving the day, he started to buckle under the strain of looking after a teenager on a daily basis. His control issues affected Erin badly. He crossed the line so much that Erin lost all respect for her father. Every event she wanted to attend or take part in, he was there in the shadows screaming at her to do better. She felt hurt and humiliated. He chose her friends, the clothes she wore and kept her away from me and her siblings. She realised that the lavish birthday parties they'd had were never attended by me or her siblings, not because we didn't want to, but because we weren't invited.

Tommy's need for control magnified and Erin lost her voice, her identity and her confidence. He broke her like he broke me. No amount of designer clothes can fix that. Everything was used as emotional blackmail. He threatened her daily with removing the things he had just bought her or that he will inform social services that she was a bad kid who would end up in a home. He rang her constantly, wanting to know her whereabouts.

The day came when he again walked in on her having a shower. She left and wouldn't return. The damage is obvious, though not to Tommy.

He violated her privacy to such an extent she is now receiving counselling from school. They rang me, concerned for her welfare and the fear she had around her own father. Eventually, she begged to come home, and I welcomed her. We might be broke, but the love she receives comes without a cost.

My brother, after years of re-enacting his own childhood of chaos and becoming an alcoholic, is now also in recovery. He is learning how to articulate emotions that he never could do until today. He is finally learning self-care on his own, away from dysfunction. Unfortunately, my sister is not ready to see the destruction she is both causing and living in, but who knows what the future holds.

I set up the ACCEPT group again and frequently meet up with Adult Children, whether they have lived with family members of addiction or any kind of abuse. They are all welcome. We are like a big family, kind and supporting of each other, sharing triumphs or tears. We listen without judgment and we watch each other unravel our confusion. We discuss what works and what doesn't, but the biggest benefit is being heard. As I grew up, I was constantly told that children should be seen and not heard. I was desperate to be heard. Hurt people hurt people. It's imperative to be heard. Cathartic.

I picked up my 9-month sober chip from AA.

Children Learn What They Live

If children live with criticism, they learn to condemn.
Hostility, they learn to fight.
Ridicule, they learn to be shy.
Shame, they learn to feel guilty.
Tolerance they learn to be patient.
Encouragement, they learn confidence.
Praise, they learn to appreciate.
Fairness, they learn justice.
Security, they learn to have faith.
Approval, they learn to like themselves.
Acceptance and friendship, they learn to find love in the world.

I studied the effects of the dynamics and family origin in dysfunctional families, toxic shame and the burdens of narcissistic parents and the roles and labels assigned to the children.

The Scapegoat: An insidious family pattern of blame and shame and abuse of a member of the family. The scapegoat child in the family is the rejected one, the one who they have chosen to abuse. One of the most painful things for a child is to be rejected and blamed, bullied and abused. The person doing the scapegoating is projecting her own inadequacy onto the scapegoat so that she doesn't have to take responsibility for her actions. Feelings of guilt, aggression, blame and suffering are projected to fulfil an unconscious drive to resolve bad feelings. The child serves as a target for blame both for the scapegoater and her supporters. Scapegoating frees the perpetrator from self-dissatisfaction and provides some narcissistic gratification to self.

Every family has its own dynamics that govern how members relate to each other. It sets the tone for how we interact with the world. In families where dysfunction is prevalent, it's not uncommon for one member to carry the blame, anger and frustration for the rest of the family. Everything is focussed on the 'troubled child.' The controller forms the narrative through lies and smear campaigns. Survivors often experience anxiety depression, poor self-esteem and blame themselves. They may eventually be diagnosed with a personality disorder and continue to have problems such as relationship issues, imposter syndrome, co-dependency, anxiety and depression. Their inner sense of self-loathing is grounded in toxic shame and they have difficulties trusting their own perceptions.

They can own their truth by reclaiming their authenticity.

The Mascot or Golden child: Initially one child is given the role of golden child. He is the parent's 'chosen one'. The golden child is seen as an extension of the narcissistic parent and the parent lives through the child. The child represents the perfect image of the parent, an extension chosen specifically for exploitation. The golden child can do no wrong, he is idolised, but at a cost. He is the parent's possession. The child is engulfed, enmeshed as one with the parent, without boundaries, and so the child may struggle to form his own identity. The expectations placed on the golden child are high, whether through social graces or performance. One of his primary jobs is to make the parent look good and to keep the parent happy. The child fears that if he can't live up to the expectations, he will lose that position and become the scapegoat. The child is imprisoned in the role of caring for the parent's needs throughout his life.

Invisible lost child: The Invisible lost child does not receive praise or blame from the parent. The child is treated as though she does not exist. She is the forgotten one, the neglected one, the unrecognized one. The narcissistic parent is not in the least bit interested or aware of this child's needs. They have absolutely no use for the child. The basic needs are ignored to varying degrees. The invisible child is treated as if she is a nobody. She grows to expect nothing nor ask for anything. She is quiet because no one is listening anyway. The child grows up finding it difficult to let others into her private world. She does not develop a healthy connection to other people, becomes lonely and isolated, but self-sufficient. The child feels unlovable and unworthy, prone to depression and may fall prey to addictive behaviours.

The invisible child's voice is lost, as are her needs. The golden child gets what she wants without having to ask and the scapegoat is always apologising for her parents' failings.

I start my day with prayer and meditation and a gratitude that I've never had before.

Today I have acceptance, I have a daily reprieve from the insidious disease of addiction and acceptance of my past.

The labels I wore are now where they were always meant to be...in the bin.

I practice self-care and self-love and keep it as simple as possible. Perfectly imperfect.

I picked up my 1-year chip from AA.

Today I am in recovery for alcohol, drugs, adrenalin, self-sabotage, borderline personality, smoking, dysfunction and I am most definitely abstaining from men, especially bad men. Did I mention men? I'm definitely abstaining from *men*!

And finally

Could I write a book? What the hell I thought, why not start and see where it goes? So, I did. With my one good hand I started to write, slowly at first and then frantically. I wrote and wrote and was astounded with the memories that came back to me. I thought about what writing would do for me and two reasons to continue became apparent; primarily to stop repeating the mistakes I was making, and secondly, perhaps my story would help another person, even if I just handed them a notebook full of my scribbles. Could I lessen their feelings of shame and inadequacy by putting my story into words?

I came across an article about a girl named Shannon Clifton, who'd had a terrible life. She was a victim of terrible sexual, mental and physical abuse at the hands of her father. She had written a book with the help of a book coach, named Ken Scott. It wasn't published at the time but was constantly referred to on social media. I decided to follow them both on social media for a few months. I dared to believe, before I approached Ken, that my scribbles were worthy of publication.

Because my judgement in the past had been so distorted and wrong, I really was trying to learn how to use my intuition, especially now that I wanted to change so badly. I was naturally wary about contacting Ken. I did a little more research on him; he was living abroad but, wow, I found out he was originally from

Newcastle! I thought that was a great sign; being a Geordie and, incidentally, he has the same name as my uncle. How weird is that? Would he be able to help me?

The real test would be when I spoke to him and so I got in touch and made some inquiries.

I felt comfortable from the start, so much so that it was like talking to an old friend that I hadn't seen in ages. He explained that not only was he looking for good material for a book, he was also looking for serious commitment. He told me bluntly, 'I only work with people who want to work hard.'

This convinced me that he was the guy to help me write my story. He informed me of the logistics, and he wanted a rough rundown of my story, condensed into a thousand words. No pressure then.

I had the thousand words to him within twenty-four hours, four hours later I got an email saying it was all systems go, he loved what I had written.

What I never expected was the genuine kind support and constant encouragement he offered throughout. I would sometimes minimise traumatic events, and Ken would then tease more out of me in a non-threatening way. He would ask questions that I hadn't thought of, which inspired further investigating on my part. The amount of penny-dropping moments I had, become incredibly cathartic for me and I knew within a chapter or two, if no one got anything from this book, at least I would.

Ken was always giving positive feedback that made me want to strive for better. Criticism and fear have always made me run a mile but, while sometimes he said my writing could improve, he gave me positive feedback and encouragement and made me strive to do well.

I loved every minute of the process, even though difficult at times, so much so that Ken never needed to push deadlines. I was always thousands of words ahead of my targets.

He genuinely wants the best for the people he helps, and I'm convinced all of them walk away with a massive sense of pride that was earned through writing about their journey. It has been a privilege to walk this path with him and I know I've made a friend for life.

Writing has been a cleansing process. It gave me the information I needed to interrupt the broken record and finally have some compassion for myself. I finally learned that other people could not give me what I needed, until I gave it to myself.

Had I not had the constant chats and prompts from my personal book coach I would have surely given up. Ken said he wouldn't allow that to happen and he meant it. He guided me through the process with enough encouragement that I found my pride and creativity once again. My confidence grew with the positive feedback and my sense of achievement has been rewarding in ways that I find almost difficult to write about.

Today I feel empowered, I feel strong and I feel sure. I know who I am and where I am going. I can live with my mistakes and not be worried that they will haunt me in the middle of the night.

My book coach guided me to find myself and encouraged me to continue when I wanted to quit. He was my godsend and for that I will forever be grateful.

Thank you, Scotty. Big love and respect for everything you do.

The end

Help lines in the UK

Domestic abuse support:
www.pennyappeal.org or 08088023333

Domestic abuse support:
www.womensaid.org

Finding Legal Options for Women Survivors:
flows.org.uk

Refuge (Women and children against domestic violence):
nationaldahelpline.org.uk or 08082000247
galop.org.uk

livefearfree.gov.uk
mensadviceline.org.uk
rapecrisis.org.uk
respectphoneline.org.uk

Alcoholics Anonymous:
help@aamail.org or 0800 9177 650

Amazon Bestseller
THE MONSTER I LOVED
The true story of a young girl and her father's betrayal
In cinemas 2021
SHANNON CLIFTON
Shannon Clifton talks about surviving her life of incest, abuse and neglect at the hands of the father she loved.

The Monster I Loved
by Shannon Clifton

Shannon Clifton has waived her right to anonymity in this highly acclaimed, dark but deeply inspiring book. Raped by her father from age six and pregnant at eleven and again at thirteen, he kidnapped her and went on the run as the net eventually closed in around him.

Shannon's story is not an easy read; she goes into graphic detail about her sexual, physical and mental abuse, which included being burned with an iron, hit with a hammer and even stabbed. Her father told her "it was something all fathers do with their daughters," and for a time she believed him.

Shannon wrote this book to start making sense of her childhood and is currently studying towards a degree in Forensic Psychology to help understand what makes people evil.

'It was a painful journey," she explains, 'but it was worth it because I want to help others who have been through similar experiences.'

Available on Amazon

Printed in Great Britain
by Amazon

53158338R00154